RAISE YOUR PROFILE, IMPACT AND INFLUENCE THROUGH SPEAKING

First published by Busybird Publishing 2019

Copyright © 2019 Mary Wong

ISBN
Print: 978-1-925949-96-4
Ebook: 978-1-925949-49-0

Mary Wong has asserted her right under the Copyright, Designs and Patents Act 1988 to be identified as the author of this work. The information in this book is based on the author's experiences and opinions. The publisher specifically disclaims responsibility for any adverse consequences, which may result from use of the information contained herein. Permission to use information has been sought by the author. Any breaches will be rectified in further editions of the book.

All rights reserved. No part of this publication may be reproduced, stored in or introduced into a retrieval system, or transmitted in any form, or by any means (electronic, mechanical, photocopying, recording or otherwise) without the prior written permission of the author. Any person who does any unauthorised act in relation to this publication may be liable to criminal prosecution and civil claims for damages. Enquiries should be made through the publisher.

Cover image: Photography: Jamie Kraus, Graphic image: Haitham L. Nahari
Cover design: Haitham L. Nahari
Layout and typesetting: Busybird Publishing

Busybird Publishing
2/118 Para Road
Montmorency, Victoria
Australia 3094

To David, Daniel and Michael, my reasons for being.

And to all who hold a desire to rise above and create an even more beautiful world.

"Men make history and not the other way around. In periods where there is no leadership, society stands still. Progress occurs when courageous, skilful leaders seize the opportunity to change things for the better."

  Harry S Truman

Contents

Acknowledgements i
Introduction v
A Note From the Author ix

Part One 1
What the Heck Does a Balloon Have to Do with Speaking? 3
The Balloon Principle Speaker Journey 9

Part Two 15
Speaking of Success 17

Part Three 31
The Balloon 33
Step One – Become Calm 35
Step Two – Acquire Skills 49
Step Three – Liberate Voice 61
Step Four – Let It Flow 69
Step Five – Own the Space 87
Step Six – Operate Devices 99
Step Seven – Nurture Progress 111

Part Four 123
Paying It Forward 125
Next Steps 129
About the Author: 131

Acknowledgements

I knew before I started that writing a book is a huge undertaking. That knowledge was part of the reason I didn't start for many years, yet this has been a far greater task than I anticipated.

This book would not be possible without the support of an enormous number of people. I wish to acknowledge some of these people – I am sure there are more!

Sally and Jason, whose belief in me started a journey many years ago from victim to victor.

My POWERtalk mentors and friends – there are so many, but in particular, Judith, who introduced me; Bernadette who is constantly the wind beneath my wings; Margaret, who is always available with superb advice and assistance; Jan, who I aspire to emulate;

Janeen, who regularly inspires me; and so many more amazing women and men who support, inspire and honestly evaluate me to help me continue to grow.

My business accountability buddy and beautiful friend, Chris Henderson – a super-star courageous woman who raises up and inspires all who know her.

My legion of beautiful friends – you know who you are – who constantly support and uplift me.

My first (and best) book coach, Megan Waldrod, who encouraged me to embrace my inner tall poppy. Megan, you are a super-star, and I cannot wait to read your book, which I know will be beyond brilliant!

My ever-patient publisher, Blaise … Thank you, over and over for being so very patient and helpful.

My brilliant graphic designer Haitham – a humble and extremely talented star.

Other book and business mentors Francesca, Natasa and Stuart, all of whom helped add propulsion to the journey.

My amazing clients and business associates – in particular, Mark, Gabrielle and Marilyn, all of whom have shown unwavering belief in my ability to continue and complete this journey.

The sensational Optimal Life Solutions team, Ruth, Karen and previously Claire, who support me by continuing to ensure the day-to-day running of the business while my head is immersed in text and the next new product.

Acknowledgements

You, the reader, for being prepared to take the step to purchase and read this book — find your voice and make a positive difference in this world and my objective will be fulfilled.

And last, but definitely not least, my incredible and very patient family, who have suffered through my constant absences, distraction, lack of hot dinners and hours in front of the computer. You are my rocks, my reason, my world.

I salute you all with love and best wishes,

Every one of you is a star.

Keep shining,

Mary xx

Introduction

"I have fought very firmly against white domination.

"I have fought very firmly against black domination.

"I cherish the idea of a new South Africa, where all South Africans are considered equal and work together..."

So stated Nelson Mandela in Kwazulu Nata in April 1994 after voting in South Africa's first democratic elections. Widely regarded as one of the greatest leaders and world-changers of all time, Mandela's journey was one of great hardship, perseverance and triumph against the odds.

When Mandela rose to speak, the world listened. *I* listened. And that was unusual, because back then, political world news was something I found extraordinarily boring – actually, I am still not a fan, but I digress.

What was it Mandela had that others didn't?

What gift allowed him to succeed where so many others had failed?

What brilliance did he embody that allowed him to engage such a following that he was able to turn the tables, bringing hope to so many in a country where hope previously did not exist?

I started to make a study – not only of Mandela, but of other speakers who changed the world. I had to know what it was that made them so great, so engaging, so powerful. At the time, I barely knew who I was and what I was about ... I was simply guided to pay attention, so I did.

About 10 years later, I started my own speaking journey when I joined POWERtalk Australia, a not-for-profit organisation that helps people gain confidence in speaking and leadership. It was around my 40th birthday and I wanted to be able to deliver a speech with ease ... which for me would mean a transition from a shaking, red-faced husky ramble to a smoothly presented message of thanks. I was terrified to stand and speak to a group of people – fearful of their judgement and concerned that I would make a fool of myself.

Fast forward 15 years. I now have a business in speaking and training. I rarely shake, get red-faced or ramble. I am often told by people that they admire my ability to speak, as they themselves find it terrifying. I always advise them that I started where they are, and the journey is simply a matter of stepping forward, one foot at a time. To start the journey, they must take the first step.

I regularly advise people to join POWERtalk Australia, which is an excellent opportunity to grow through participation and feedback.

This book includes some of what I have learnt over my years of studying speakers, practicing speaking and being mentored by some of the world's best speakers; and is underpinned by my many years of formal study into counselling, coaching, business and leadership.

It is geared to serve those who wish to deliver a message that engages a following in a sustainable business model. I ask that you use it ethically, honestly and with passion to bring about a legacy of positive change for this world. I do so because I know I don't have all the answers our planet needs now, but I am sure the answers are out there, waiting to be shared, to be enacted, to come to fruition; and I want my legacy to be one of empowering the visionary change-leaders to have the power, influence and impact that they need to deliver their legacy.

A Note From the Author

So, you want to change the world?

You want to be influential, to have impact, a high profile?

No doubt, you have already had conversations that go a little like this ...

"Really? Who do you think you are?"

"What makes you think your idea will work when so many others haven't?"

"Yeah? You and what army?"

It's quite likely that you may have even had those conversations with yourself!

I'm here to tell you that you **can** do this! It's achievable, provided you keep at it and make sure you have the skills and knowledge to grow your 'army' of followers and supporters. You can even make money at the same time.

I often find those with a vision for positive change have a mindset that doesn't really include making money. So, let's address that elephant right from the start.

Whether you are planning to take the not-for-profit pathway or the business pathway, money is necessary in order to sustain your mission. That doesn't mean if you don't have millions you won't make it.

What it means is that when you plan your journey, it is vital to plan how to make money along the way, and to do it in a way that creates passive income (i.e. income that creates more income without needing more effort). You may start with assistance, but sponsorship is not a sustainable model. Generosity has its limits. The passing on or change of circumstances for a major donor can bring a sponsored project to an abrupt halt.

A big-picture vision is needed when planning for lasting impact. A business or organisation without sustainably sourced and projected income targets is a business or organisation planning to fail.

In this book I will share some of the tips and methods that have worked both for me and fellow industry professionals who have consulted me for advice.

Of course, it's time to insert the disclaimer. I am neither a financial planner, nor a financial adviser. I absolutely recommend you seek qualified advice in this area.

A Note From the Author

Please consider your own position and seek advice from your planner and/or finance team to ensure these are a fit for you before implementing them into your plan.

My areas of expertise are speaking and leadership. As a professional speaker and trainer, I will share with you the professional secrets on sharing a message, raising your profile, engaging your following and leaving a lasting impact. I will do this using my signature speaking system – the Balloon Principle®.

What the Heck Does a Balloon Have to Do with Speaking?

> "I think I will be able to, in the end, rise above the clouds and climb the stairs to Heaven, and I will look down on my beautiful life."
>
> **Yayoi Kusama**

I don't know where my fear of heights started. I have childhood memories of jumping from the car roof to the ground (and from the veranda roof) with the words "tell my mum I wasn't afraid to do it!" I have no idea what that was about, but I recall feeling (reasonably) anxious about jumping from a height more than twice (or thrice) my own body height.

My next memory of fear of heights was at age 17, when I commenced nursing training. We had to move into the nurses' quarters and the Preliminary Nursing Course students were housed on the top floor – a whole four stories up in the air. While that may not sound like much, to a small-town country girl who had never been more than one floor up from the ground, that felt like a very long way up! As I exited the lift with my suitcase, I looked across the foyer to the French doors that opened onto a balcony, surrounded by a solid concrete balustrade with steel railing on top. The balcony was easily three metres wide. Some of my compatriots were sitting on top of the concrete, swinging their legs between the rail and looking down. I froze. They called me out to join them, but I could not go. To this day, my stomach sinks when I think about them – I was sure they would fall and couldn't look. It took several months before I could walk onto the balcony, and I never came close to looking over the balustrade, let alone sitting on it!

That was 1982. In 2016, I fulfilled a long-held dream to travel to South Africa, accompanied by my husband and two sons. While there, we were fortunate to be able to spend time at Pilanesberg National Park. My husband, as spouses sometimes do, got the fabulous idea that we should do something memorable while we were there (as if being on safari wasn't memorable enough) and booked a hot air balloon ride for the two of us. Originally, he wanted to take the boys too. They weren't keen and I convinced him not to push as it was a lot of money, and they'd be able to pay their own way when they were ready. But I was lying! The money was not the issue – the reality was that I was sure I would be curled up in foetal position on the bottom of the basket, screaming and crying, and I didn't want my boys to see that.

We booked to fly several days ahead of our departure and were told we could only fly if the wind conditions were suitable. Our flight was cancelled four times, before, to my dismay, on our last day in the park, we were advised we would be flying.

On the way to the balloon, there was an incident where our open-topped safari vehicle was surrounded by lions. We were advised to stay still and silent. It was deeply concerning but paled in significance to my fear of the flight.

There were 10 people in the balloon – eight guests and two operators. The basket was separated into sections – a circular section in the centre housed the gas burner and the operators, and the remainder of the basket that was sectioned into four parts, with two guests in each part. It was quite a squeeze – foetal position on the floor was not an option. I had to face my fear and rise with the balloon.

As I stood, breathless with a pounding heart, posing for photographs with a grimace of fear (which could have been considered a smile, if one didn't know better), a loud noise behind me attracted my attention. It was the gas firing under the balloon. I gazed in awe at the colourful silk canopy, wondering how I would cope with lift-off once it came, then looked back to the outside. To my amazement, the thing I had been so worried about had happened already – we were about 3 metres off the ground!

I gulped. My heart missed some beats. Then I made a choice. I had no control over the balloon, but I did have control over my response to the situation, so I made a conscious decision to just enjoy the flight.

The Balloon Principle

I am sure the flight will remain one of the highlights of my life – we effortlessly and majestically glided across the lake through the sunrise watching hippos, elephants, giraffes, wildebeest, impala, rhinos, warthogs and even a brown hyaena loping along the ridge on the horizon. The only time I felt at all concerned for my safety was when we were landing into a clearing surrounded by men with big guns – they were there to scare off lions in case one suddenly appeared from behind a bush, intent on grabbing a quick breakfast.

I was absolutely exhilarated! Joyously, we celebrated over a champagne breakfast, before reluctantly heading back to our hotel to pack.

On the flight home I had plenty of time for reflection. It felt surreal. Had I really done this thing? *Yes.*

If I had the chance would I do it again? *Um ... maybe? I think, perhaps? Um ... why not? Gee, I'm still a bit scared ...*

I had done it, and it was wonderful, but I really wasn't sure I could do it again. I examined my reaction. Could it be because it still felt like a dream? Did I just not believe it happened? Why was I choosing to step back into a fear I had already conquered – even if it was only for 30 minutes or so? Did I *need* to do it again to prove to myself it had happened? I meditated, allowing myself to be back in the balloon. Again, I felt the serene majesty of a floating high over the African plains. Again, I felt the peace of freedom from fear. I decided to simply sit with it for a while to allow it to feel more real and went on with my life.

A couple of years later, assisting clients with their fear of speaking, I used the balloon trip as a metaphor; explaining the technique of choosing to let go of fear.

It resonated so well, that I brought it into my courses as a regular story.

Then, one day, I had a huge realisation.

I realised that the speaker's journey from timid beginner to polished professional was reflective of the balloon ride. I further realised that the balloon 'principle' was applicable in any circumstance where fear is holding us back. I applied my learnings from the balloon ride to my training in speaking and the Balloon Principle was born.

The Balloon Principle Speaker Journey

This illustration shows the speaker's journey.

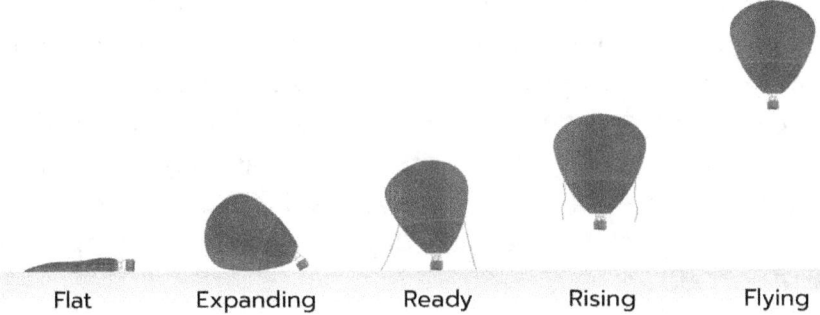

Flat: We start our journey as a nervous new speaker, like an uninflated balloon – no skills, no confidence, no hot air. Fear stops us from going further. This is the most vital point – it is at this point that the first step must be taken. We can decide in this space to wait, or to take the step. Too often, at this point, a choice is made to pack it all up and go in a different direction. The hopes, dreams and aspirations of the budding speaker are shelved, stored away or discarded until, sometimes years later, the balloon is again unpacked and meticulously laid out in preparation for that vital first step. I encourage you to take the first step. The consequences of not doing so can be detrimental to your sense of self-worth.

Expanding: We've taken the first step. Now, we start to learn. We do some classes, give it a go, start to grow. We do our first speech – for some of us, the first time we have stood in front of a group in many years. We are wobbly, shaky, struggling and nervous. Our confidence cup needs some topping up. And all of that is OK, because we have at least taken the first step. Doing so makes us feel both proud and terrified! Now, it's time to keep stepping.

Often, I meet people who tell me they cannot speak in public – they've tried, and it was all too awful, so they haven't tried again. Choosing to stop when you are feeling uncomfortable can leave you with a belief that you are not capable. The truth is, learning is often uncomfortable. If you embrace the discomfort, put in the time and effort and allow yourself space to practice, the discomfort will lessen and you will discover that you *can* do it!

Ready: The journey continues. We allow ourselves opportunities to speak, to get feedback, we learn some more and we start to improve. We have the skills and the ability. We may find ourselves at a point where the symptoms of nervousness are no longer obvious when we get up to speak. We need to keep up the practice and find new larger audiences. We are ready to take this to the next level – to step it up and make it professional. But something is stopping us – our guide ropes are still attached.

For some of us, the thing stopping us is not knowing how to step out into the public, where to get opportunities, how to get paid. For some, it is the fear of being seen, of letting people know our inner essence, of speaking our truth. Either way, we are in a comfort zone that needs to be breached! It's time to find the way out.

Rising: We step out of our comfort zone and start to accept unpaid or low-paying gigs in public. We may even start to run our own workshops or events to allow ourselves a space to speak, to share our message. We learn to refine content according to the audience we are speaking with. We are getting runs on the board, becoming known. Our confidence cup is getting fuller and fuller and we are lapping it up. It's early days, and our guide ropes are trailing – they are our safety net, there to help us to keep rising.

In this space, you must ensure you are surrounded with support. Mentoring is a vital factor in continuing to rise. You must maintain a strong mindset; a deep sense of belief in yourself and your vision. Keep your eyes on the prize and continue to rise.

Flying: Suddenly, we are there. High-flying, majestic, serene. We intuitively seem to know how to move a crowd, how to communicate with them on a very deep level, and we can manoeuvre our planned talk to make it work regardless of unexpected circumstances. We are calm, confident and in control. We are in the big leagues, giving a stand-out performance – it's hypnotic! Our confidence cup is full and when we reflect on the journey, we sometimes feel we should pinch ourselves to believe we are truly here.

It's interesting to note here that when you look at the journey illustration, the first three stages are all on the same level. As one progresses through those stages, one may often feel like they are making little or no progress despite the time and effort being applied to the process.

It can be an uncomfortable time. That's the thing about learning new stuff. Realising that we are in new and unfamiliar territory can make us feel a bit lost, and nobody likes that feeling. Remember, embrace the discomfort – for when you feel discomfort, you are growing. As you grow, you will again become comfortable, until eventually you will look back and wonder what it was that worried you, because it will become second nature.

The really fun thing about life is that each time you feel you have learnt all there is to know about something, you discover something else, something new you don't know. Regardless of where we are on the journey, every one of us has more to learn. There is always another lesson, another path to take.

So even when you get to fly, there will be times of discomfort. The way you deal with those times will define you as a leader and a speaker. We are defined by the way we get back up, not the way we fall. So, when things go awry, have a laugh, get back up, stand strong, and move forward ... That is the essence of confidence.

The Balloon Principle Speaker Journey

Reflection

Where do you sit in the speaking journey?

What next step could you take to move forward?

Is there something stopping you?

What support could you put in place to assist you?

Who could you reach out to for mentoring?

Action

Identify where you are now, what is holding you back and decide what first step you can take to move you past it. Then, take that step.

Part Two

Speaking of Success

> *"You don't have to be great at something to start, but you have to start to be great at something."*
> **Zig Ziglar**

In any pathway, success is an individual destination. It is no different for a speaker. For one person, success might mean speaking at an event with 100 people. For another it might be 1000. For another it might be an online summit with 100 000 or more tuning in. It's important to define what success means to you, so you know what your targeted destination is – without that definition you are a ship without a rudder, sailing wherever the wind may take you. When defining this intention, consider your vision and the legacy you wish to leave for the world.

But a destination is not all that is required. You need to set a pathway – a map to follow for your journey. You map should include short-term, medium-term and longer-term aspirations as well as the big picture intention. When defining these, they must be specific, detailed, time-framed and realistically attainable and they must serve you and your vision.

Once you have set these intentions, it is time to work towards them. There are certain keys to attaining success as a speaker. While there are other small things that will require attention, these are the five main keys to success. Persistently and consistently attend to these keys, and the other smaller things that arise will fall into place as you go along.

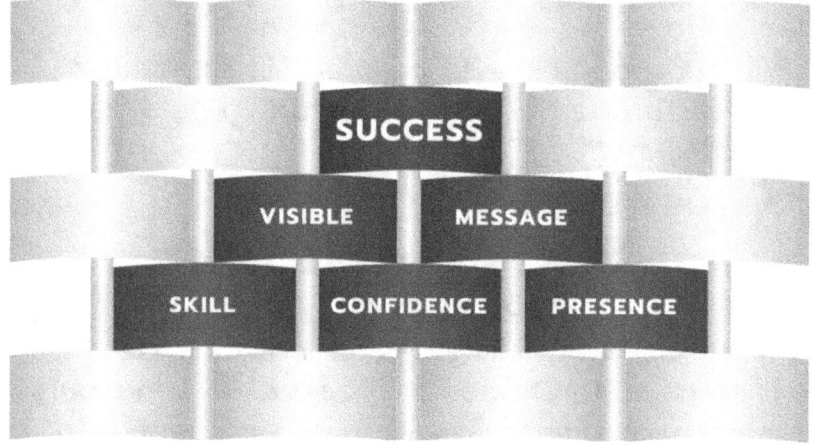

Skill

In your industry:

Have you ever listened to a speaker and found they had no substance to their claims or that they lacked credibility because they didn't have the knowledge to back them up? It's an issue I see all too regularly in the speaking business.

It is important to recognise that formal research is never based on a single experience. If something worked for you, it doesn't mean it will work for everyone. Before you start telling people that you have the cure they've been looking for, you must research and formally test your theory to back-up your claims.

One of the first things I always recommend to people wanting to speak on a subject is to make sure they have done enough research in addition to their lived experience. Anecdotes will not suffice and should be used only to engage listeners or embed learning through the power of story. Your credibility will be questioned if you are unable to give empirical proof of your theories; or, if you are unable to disprove existing published research with your analytical research.

In your ability to connect:

One of the greatest skills any human can use as a speaker is the ability to connect deeply with their audience. To achieve this, the speaker must show their audience respect by ensuring they listen to connect, then find common ground from which to build their dialogue.

The first step in this process is the building of trust with the audience. I will address this in greater depth in Step 5 – Own the Space.

One of the things that can get in the way of building rapport is an over-inflated ego. The role of ego in speaking is commonly misunderstood. Ego does play a role in the life of a speaker – it must be strong enough for the speaker to be resilient in the face of adversity e.g. low attendance or income when first starting out. But when speaking to a group, one must put their ego aside. If you are not prepared to listen and learn from the people to whom you speak, you will not gain their respect. Respect must be earned in the rapport building process and maintained throughout your presentation.

In your ability to communicate your message:

Some people appear to be born with a gift for communication. For those who struggle to clearly express a concept, this can be deflating. We assume that it should all occur naturally, but why should it when we are born unable to speak at all? Our ability to express thoughts and communicate needs is learned from shared experiences as we grow. It is quite likely that those with an apparent gift were immersed in a culture of communicative excellence from an early age. For the rest of us, not having been exposed to excellence in communication in our formative years, it is unlikely that it will come naturally.

I know from my own personal experience that excellence in communication can be learned, regardless of how challenged you may be. My communication improvement journey started when I studied nursing. It was mind-boggling to me that there were actual techniques one could use when conversing with someone to open up a conversation.

At that time, I had never heard of open-ended questions, or the SOLER model (see illustration) and for the most part, I found a one on one conversation very challenging. I felt awkward and inept when in groups or at parties, because I didn't know what to say or how to say it. I avoided speaking up on issues or problems that arose because I had no idea how to approach the subject.

> **THE SOLER EFFECTIVE COMMUNICATION MODEL**
>
> Designed in 1986 by Gerald Egan to describe five key components of active listening
>
> **S** Sit **squarely** facing each other – indicates you are focused on them
>
> **O** Maintain an **open** posture – indicates you are open to converse
>
> **L** **Lean** in towards each other – indicates interest
>
> **E** Establish **eye** contact – indicates respect and listening
>
> **R** Be **relaxed** in your posture – helps them be more relaxed
>
> Egan, G. (1986), 'The Skilled Helper', 3rd Ed., Brooks/Cole, Belmont, California.

Applying my newly learned techniques when speaking with patients was a valuable improvement but my problems persisted in social and personal situations. My issues were deeply rooted in my sub-conscious – a result of childhood bullying and one particularly traumatic childhood incident.

My amygdala was in hijack in group situations and I had to get help to decompress the effects in order to remove the block. I sought psychological assistance and was able to move past it. The sense of liberation in having passed through and out the other side of social anxiety is phenomenal. I encourage anyone with social anxiety to seek professional help – you won't be sorry you did.

My fascination for learning communication continued. Studying counselling added several more communication skills, and I have since studied several concepts for clarifying messages. I am certified in Conversational Intelligence® and HBDI® for whole brain communications. I have studied Crucial Communications®, having attended courses in person, and have participated for more than 30 years in workshops and activities presented from experts in the field in the area of communication.

The techniques shared in my workshops and in Step 3 – Liberate Voice as part of the balloon principle were created using an integrative approach, incorporating factors from my studies and 50+ years life experience.

Presence

Think of the great leaders you have watched captivate their audience. One thing you will notice if you watch them is that they have charisma – that special something that draws people towards them, and has their audience wishing for more.

One of the things I am constantly asked is how to 'own the floor' as a position of authority. While growing presence is a difficult concept to explain, there are certain attributes that will make you more believable as a leader.

Here's a quick list. You'll find more on this in Step 5 - Own the Space

- Be respectful of all people, even those you disagree with.
- Be prepared to listen, connect deeply and take the time to make the audience feel valued.
- Love yourself, but keep your ego in check.
- Get to know yourself intimately – investigate your values and beliefs and live in alignment with them.

- Define your vision and mission.
- Commit to excellence, hard work and integrity.
- Help the room understand what to expect.
- Deliver on stated expectations.
- Be open to new ideas.
- Communicate in a whole brain model so you reach every person's processing style.
- Answer questions truthfully, without avoidance tactics.
- Be truthful always.
- Radiate love.
- Show genuine warmth and compassion.
- Be prepared to have the hard conversations and do so with grace.
- Pay attention to the responses of your audience.
- Be supportive and encouraging of all around you.
- Practise non-judgement.
- Learn how to be persuasive and have a call to action.
- Stand strong in the face of objection.
- Lead by example.
- Be resilient.
- Don't take yourself too seriously.
- Laugh.
- Share your wisdom to help others.

And the biggest one of all... BE YOU! I am certain that the biggest creator of charisma is being 100% true to yourself, your values, your beliefs, your personality and all your uniqueness.

Visibility

Being authentic, true to who you are and what you believe is of great benefit to establishing yourself as a credible leader. You never know who is looking, so take care to walk your talk (e.g. if you are an ecowarrior, you need to be taking care of the environment at home, not just when you are in the public eye).

Live true to your values and beliefs, and you will find peace and the ability to love yourself. Once you love yourself, you become less worried about sharing from your heart, allowing your impact as a speaker to grow exponentially.

On my journey, I was afraid to be seen for many years – a traumatic experience as a child and being branded as a liar in the aftermath left me believing that nobody would believe what I had to say – that I wasn't worthy to have my own opinion or stories. It wasn't until I was able to get past that belief, that I rose as a professional speaker. I was doing ok – I had made it to the top level of international trainers, but I didn't move a crowd the way I wanted to.

My impact and influence were lacking. When I was able to accept, love and BE myself, my star rose. I see audience members mesmerised and sometimes tearing up when I share stories. I know my words touch them deeply.

Being visible involves being unafraid to be seen – not just on the outside, but also allowing your innermost thoughts and feelings to come to the surface, so others see the real essence of who you are. That is where your power lies.

When you get to the point where you are unafraid to be seen, it's time to gain attention. You can start to appear on Social Media, events, live-streaming, traditional media, or anywhere else where there are people looking and listening. At this point it is vital you can answer questions with ease and authority and speak off-the-cuff.

A smooth, well-delivered measured response to a question screams confidence. Again, POWERtalk Australia is a brilliant place to learn how to do this, as each meeting includes impromptu speaking sessions in which to practice. You'd be surprised how helpful that is.

Message

Before you can deliver a well-structured, clear and credible message, it is imperative you know what you stand for. Refine your vision and mission and put in place a mission statement which rings true in all that you do. Live in accordance with the mission and vision, and you will be able to structure a message that fits them.

When you speak, select opportunities that are true to your cause. Take care to use story that fits the message, and is relevant to the audience, otherwise it is simply an indulgence. We all have plenty of stories to share, so be prepared to keep some for another occasion.

Structure your message in a way that serves your audience. When speaking, the audience does not have the benefit of a written article to follow. If your information is not simply structured with clear and concise facts, you will need audio-visual assistance to prevent your information getting lost. PowerPoint presentations are excellent for reinforcing a point through visual diagrams such as Venn Diagrams, timelines, graphs and charts. Remember though, that the slideshow is the back-up singer and you are the main event.

It is not necessary to have every word of your presentation on PowerPoint slides (in fact, it's boring and an insult to your audience's intelligence) and please, do not read your presentation off the slide show.

Recently I watched a sales presentation by someone who charges nearly $500 an hour for their services in coaching. She read her entire presentation – even the slides that explained what she did in her sessions.

She did not get one shred of interest in her services – after all, who would pay $500 an hour for someone who couldn't tell you what they would do in that hour without reading it off a screen? I know I wouldn't! She lost all credibility by reading her slides.

Confidence

Out of all the keys to successful speaking, this attribute is most important. If you cannot confidently deliver a message about your product or idea, it looks as though you don't believe in it. And that will not gain you sponsorship, support or sales. But where do you find confidence?

Self-development is a huge part of becoming confident. Knowing, accepting and loving yourself, regardless of your so-called flaws (I prefer to consider them areas for growth) helps you to stand tall and confidently.

Mindset is also a very large part of confidence and a term you will hear over and over in business and self-development. But what exactly is Mindset?

The term refers to the way you speak to yourself – the way in which you set your mind to things. At any moment, in any situation, you can choose your response to circumstances. For example, prior to speaking to a group, you can choose to ignore the voices that say 'do you really think you can do this? Who do you think you are? What have you got to offer?' You can choose to ignore them, or you can choose to answer them with all manner of answers.

Your answer could be a strong positive affirmation such as "I am a born leader, with a big mission which I will today confidently and calmly convey to this group of enthusiastic learners."

Your answer could be a less strong, but equally powerful affirmation such as "I am a lifelong learner, having a positive learning experience by sharing information with a group of intelligent fellow-learners. Our experience will be one of sharing knowledge and I am open to learning from them just as they are open to learning from me."

Your answer could be "I'm having a panic attack and want to leave now. I have little to offer."

Which answer would serve you better?

The choice of answer is up to you! See STEP 1 - BECOME CALM for more information about how we speak with ourselves when under duress.

The Balloon Principle

Allowing yourself to step into situations of discomfort, or challenge, is one of the biggest confidence-growing activities you can do. For some, this takes a dive in the deep end, for others, baby steps are needed. Take the time to work out what works best for you and start doing it! The size of the step is not what matters. What matters is that you take the step.

Reflection

What does success look like for you (your final intention)?

What are your short-term aspirations?

What are your medium-term aspirations?

What are your long-term aspirations?

What key elements do you already have? What ones do you need to work on?

What is your preferred rate of growth — baby steps or deep-end plunge??

Action

Set a pathway towards your vision.

Draw or write your pathway into a visual plan.

At one side, list the five keys, along with a checklist of areas in which to grow.

Prioritise those growth areas and get to work.

If you are socially anxious, seek psychological help and be freed from the grip.

Consider engaging a coach to help you if you have difficulty in mapping your journey.

Join a local POWERtalk Australia club if you need opportunities to improve your confidence in speaking to groups and answering off-the-cuff. Find your local club at this link:

www.powertalkaustralia.org.au/find-a-club-near-you

Part Three

The Balloon

> *"Enjoy your sweat because hard work doesn't guarantee success, but without it you don't have a chance."*
> **Alex Rodriguez**

The steps along the journey of the Balloon Principle speaker form the acronym Balloon and are shown on the illustrations (left).

These steps are as follows:

- Become Calm
- Acquire Skills
- Liberate Voice
- Let it Flow
- Own the Space
- Operate Devices
- Nurture Progress

Let's visit each step and discuss the work that needs to happen in each step so you can become the polished professional speaker you want to be.

Step One

Become Calm

> "I learned that courage was not the absence of fear, but the triumph over it. The brave man is not he who does not feel afraid, but he who conquers that fear."
> **Nelson Mandela**

No matter what stage you are at in life, there will be moments in time when you feel fear – whether you recognise it as fear or not. Our bodies are hard-wired to respond to stimulus with bodily reactions and raised adrenaline levels.

This has served our human race since the beginning of time, by keeping us safe from danger. We learned what was dangerous and embedded our learnings in our most primitive part of our brain, the amygdala.

When we find ourselves in a dangerous situation, our amygdala lights up, and triggers a response throughout our body to prepare us for whatever action may need to be taken to make us safe and keep us alive.

This response includes a boost to our adrenaline levels in our body – adrenaline being the hormone responsible for raised heartbeat, tight chest, shaking, dry mouth, nausea, red face, and pupil dilation, to name but a few.

You will no doubt have heard of the fight or flight response where you either stop and fight, or you run away. From my analysis, I believe there are four responses, not two.

Fight – stand and fight.

Flee – run away.

Freeze – stand completely still, like a deer in the headlights.

Flop – drop dead, pass out or faint.

As a speaker, none of those is an acceptable response to being called out to the front of the room. We need to have strategies in place to assist us to lower our adrenaline levels so we can perform at our best. I say 'lower' our levels, not remove the hormone all together, because a slightly elevated adrenalin level can work to our advantage, adding energy and stamina, thus improving our performance.

In this chapter, I will advise on how to regulate our adrenaline levels, give specific tips to alleviate the symptoms of fear, and assist you with strategies to remain calm when speaking.

A word about fear:

We have been conditioned to believe that fear is our foe, but the truth is that fear is our friend. Fear is there to protect us, to keep us safe. In positions of great peril, our ancient programs remind us that we must step carefully, and adrenaline kicks in to give us the boost we need to get to safety. This serves us well when we are in actual physical danger. The problem is, there are times when the bodily response is out of proportion to the level of danger.

Logically, we know just speaking is not dangerous, yet our bodies respond as though it is. If you think about, it you will realise it is not actually speaking that we fear most. It is being judged – and found unworthy to remain part of the collective. This response dates to caveman days when, if we did something that separated us from the group, we were at high risk of death by being eaten or starving.

So, if we are not going to starve or become some wild animal's dinner, we need to find ways to manage the body's response to the perceived danger. The first step is to recognise that we are simply having a bodily reaction to something that is not actually dangerous and name it for what it is – an irrational fear response.

Secondly, and very importantly, we need to not judge ourselves for feeling it – our body is just doing its job. When we judge ourselves harshly, we add a larger cortisol response that just makes things worse. Instead, aim love at yourself and thank your body for doing its job. When we accept, rather than fighting something, it takes away the angst, and adds ease to the process of managing the situation.

Managing Adrenaline

Just as your body is equipped with all it needs to add adrenaline, it also holds what it needs to settle it down again. The parasympathetic nervous system works specifically to conserve energy, producing a calm and relaxed feeling in the mind and body when it is activated. It is the antithesis of the adrenaline response, so to manage our adrenaline levels, all we need to do is activate our parasympathetic nervous system.

One of the best ways to do that, is to breathe – not the shallow breaths we tend to do when we are afraid, though. Deep abdominal breaths move the vagus nerve, stimulating the parasympathetic nervous system, and targeting specific muscles in the heart, resulting in lower heart rate and decreased blood pressure. A minimum of three deep breaths is required to start the process. My recommendation is five to ten breaths, to make sure it is well and truly working.

It's perhaps surprising that most of us do not know how to perform deep abdominal breathing. We are conditioned to believe that our abdomens should always remain tense and tightly tucked in. To abdominally breathe, we must relax these muscles and allow the abdomen to expand. Take a deep breath in, allowing it to pass all the way down through your heart to your stomach area, and allow your lungs to fill completely with air. Your shoulders should not move upwards, and your stomach should move outwards.

It's useful to know how to breathe abdominally, as this technique is an excellent stress reliever, useful not only when speaking but in any time of stress. If you are going through a particularly difficult time or are aware that you are in a stressful situation, I recommend you set an hourly alarm during the day and perform a minimum of five abdominal breaths each hour. You will be surprised at how effective it is.

When the adrenaline gets out of control.

Sometimes breathing is not enough. If you are one of those people for whom the thought of standing to speak sends you into panic, there are advanced options for calming yourself. In my counselling training I learnt meditation and grounding practices and have put them to use many times for assisting people caught in fear and panic.

Even if you don't go into panic at the thought of speaking, meditation is useful for clearing your mind and calming yourself prior to a speaking engagement. You will engage your audience far more quickly if you enter the room relaxed and happy. See STEP FIVE - OWNING THE SPACE

I have designed a grounding meditation to use specifically for speaking. My clients swear by it and I personally find it useful in any situation where I feel challenged. I recommend you practice it daily for a minimum 30 days. After this you will find you are able to get yourself into a space of calm in a very short time — I can do it in a matter of seconds now. It's a very powerful tool and you can download it free by contacting me directly via the contact form on my website www.optimalcoaching.com.au

Those words in your head

In addition to breathing and meditation, it is imperative you manage your thoughts. Nothing brings you undone faster than negative self-talk. Our thoughts affect our feelings, then our feelings affect our behaviour, which then reinforces our thoughts – it is a vicious cycle that will continue if we don't interrupt the pattern and change our thoughts.

Many self-development gurus recommend using a positive affirmation – and if that works for you, go right ahead! What I have noticed in my coaching work with clients is that most tell me that positive affirmations don't work for them, as they don't really believe the words.

I am a great believer in reframing of negative words – I personally have experienced the power of a good reframe. But I also remember how difficult it can be when you first start out putting reframes and positive affirmations in place. It's a big jump from "I can't" to "I can", particularly if you don't yet have the skills you need.

If you truly don't believe the affirmation, you will reject it subconsciously and it will do more harm than good to blithely tell yourself you can do this thing. My recommendation is to take baby steps, rather than a quantum leap. Start by adding the word 'yet' to your negative self-talk. "I can't do this" becomes "I can't do this yet" and adds a sense of possibility, opening you mind up to trying, rather than being defeated. Then after a while, you will move to "I'm getting better at this every time I practice it" and eventually, "I can do this" happens as if by magic.

I recommend you seek a mentor on this journey - someone who supports you and advocates for your ability to the negative voices in your head. Having a voice of experience to run through things makes it much easier. We all think we are the only one to go through our journey. We assume that people who speak comfortably were never nervous, but that is rarely the case. Share your journey with someone who knows it intimately – they will help you leap-frog over issues as they arise.

Pro-Tips

Even the most experienced speakers will occasionally have an irrational fear response in their bodies. To manage these responses, here are some pro-tips that may help.

Dry mouth

- I remember attending a keynote address at a conference where the speaker was being paid the big dollars, but there was no water. He got nervous and couldn't continue because his mouth was too dry. He asked for water, then stood near the lectern for 10 minutes waiting for the water before continuing. It took quite a deal of time for him to win back his audience, who disengaged while he stood unable to speak. A lesson here for both organisers and speakers – remember to make sure you have a glass of water available when you speak.
- When using a glass, pick it up while speaking, and hold it a short time. When you come to the end of the sentence, pause and take a sip. Then continue to hold it for a short time. If you need another sip, you can take another between sentences before purposefully putting it back down in another pause. Looking relaxed while holding the glass is key here. Rushing to pick up a glass, take a sip,

then replace the glass is not only ungainly but can bring you undone, splashing water on yourself, your notes, your equipment or even on the floor which can lead to bigger calamities when you slip in it accidentally later in your presentation. Take your time and you will look far more professional, without the potential problems.

- There is a current trend towards using water bottles, but my perception is that this does not look professional. Always be aware of the perceptions of your audience – something as small as drinking from a bottle can lower their opinion of you as a speaker.
- Think of something very sour. Tamarind always works for me - just the thought and I'm drooling like Beasley the Dog in the 1989 movie, Turner and Hooch. (Fabulous movie – if you have never seen it, do yourself a favour and find a copy!) If you've never tasted tamarinds, find someone with a tamarind tree and taste a fresh one – the bottled paste is nowhere near as sharp, and won't leave a lasting impression. Failing that, think grapefruit, lemon or any other flavour sour enough to make you wink, and your salivary glands will activate.
- Another way to activate the salivary glands and moisten the mouth is to move your tongue rapidly from side to side across the back of your upper teeth. This gives your sublingual salivary gland a good massage and results in the release of saliva, moistening the mouth. The good thing is it can be done in front of an audience while pausing, without them realising you are doing anything at all.

Crying

- There are times when sharing emotional material onstage can make us tear-up. There's nothing wrong with showing emotion – in fact it adds impact to your presentation when you can do this without it affecting your ability to speak. Don't be afraid to show emotion – not showing it can make you seem like a robot, or unbelievable.
- Particularly emotional times, such as delivering a eulogy – require added assistance. When you sob or gasp, it is very difficult to speak or enunciate clearly. To remedy this, push your tongue hard up against the roof of your mouth and take a very deep breath. Nobody will judge you for taking the time to steady yourself – they're all wondering how you found the strength to stand and speak at such a time, so they'll applaud your ability.
- Another technique that works is to pinch the skin between your thumb and your index finger. This is an acupressure point and assists to regulate your parasympathetic nervous system.

Husky voice, tightness or lump in the throat

- Tightness in the throat is usually due to tensing the muscles around the face and mouth. Make a conscious effort to relax your muscles – you might tense them deliberately first for the count of three, so you find it easier to relax them.
- Yawning also helps to release throat and face muscles and makes the voice less husky.

The Balloon Principle

- Preparation for your voice is important. Lip bubbling (also known as blowing raspberries) is an excellent exercise for relaxing muscles in preparation, although not something that can be done on stage.
- A sip of water also comes in handy here (see dry mouth above)

Shaking or swaying

- This is a result of too much adrenaline. Make sure you follow the adrenaline steps as mentioned previously. Also, remember to use the right words in your head. Embrace the fear – fear is your friend. Stop fighting it and you will discover how it helps you.
- If your legs are shaking, it is quite likely that you are standing on the ball of your foot. Allow your feet to be shoulder width apart, knees straight but not full-lock, and stand strong with your weight over your heels. Imagine a ball in your stomach, with roots going down your legs and into the floor. You will feel strong, invincible. The shaking may not go entirely, but the added strength will allow you to continue without looking like you are about to run offstage.
- If you are swaying, that is a result of not standing evenly through both feet simultaneously. Stand strong, and the sway will leave you.
- Remember to make your movements purposeful. Don't pace about the stage for no reason. Being prepared to stand still and calmly claim the space will add to your charisma. If you are going to move, make it more than just one step – single steps make you look frightened.

- When your hands are shaking, do not hold a sheet of paper. Use a lectern or table to put your paper on, and rest your hand there, with the palm open and downwards. There is a tendency in this situation to grasp the side of the lectern or table. This conveys nervousness to your audience and is not recommended.
- A gentle massage in the muscle area between the thumb and index finger can help to relieve shakiness.

For many years I let fear hold me back. At age 11, there was an incident where I had guns held to my head. In the aftermath, I was labelled a liar, and left thinking nobody would even believe what I had to say. I lived in fear for many years before rediscovering my voice and allowing myself to live my truth. What I discovered when I eventually got past my fear is that we have a choice. We can let fear have power over us, or we can let fear give us power. Fear is a part of life. Without it, courage does not exist.

I encourage you to take the steps required to become calm and move forward. I believe that if you have a message that will benefit our world, then your mission is bigger than your fear. Step into it, lean into the fear and let it support you. You can do this. You are braver than you know.

Reflection

On a scale of 1 – 10 where 1 is not at all fearful and 10 is very fearful, where would you rate your fear of speaking?

What happens to your body when you stand to speak?

What thoughts go through your mind when you think about speaking?

Who could you ask to be your mentor?

What other action could you take to challenge yourself, so you grow stronger

Action

Write your negative thoughts in a journal and reframe them into a more positive statement that resonates with you. Write that statement on a whiteboard, mirror or window with whiteboard marking pen and read it regularly. When you can own that statement, step it up with a new more positive statement. Allow yourself to grow in steps.

Rate your fear level and plot it on a chart. Give yourself opportunities to regulate your adrenaline through progressive challenges. After a month, rate your fear again. Continue to chart the fear rating monthly along your speaking journey – you will be surprised how quickly it drops.

Find a tamarind tree and try a fresh tamarind.

Watch Turner and Hootch (just for fun!).

Step Two
Acquire Skills

"Skill and confidence are an unconquered army."
　George Herbert

Competence and Its Effect on Our Confidence

The model of conscious and unconscious competence was first described by Martin M. Broadwell as "the four levels of teaching" in February 1969.

The model describes learning a new skill as consisting of four stages, progressing from unconscious incompetence to unconscious competence as demonstrated in the illustration (overleaf).

The Balloon Principle

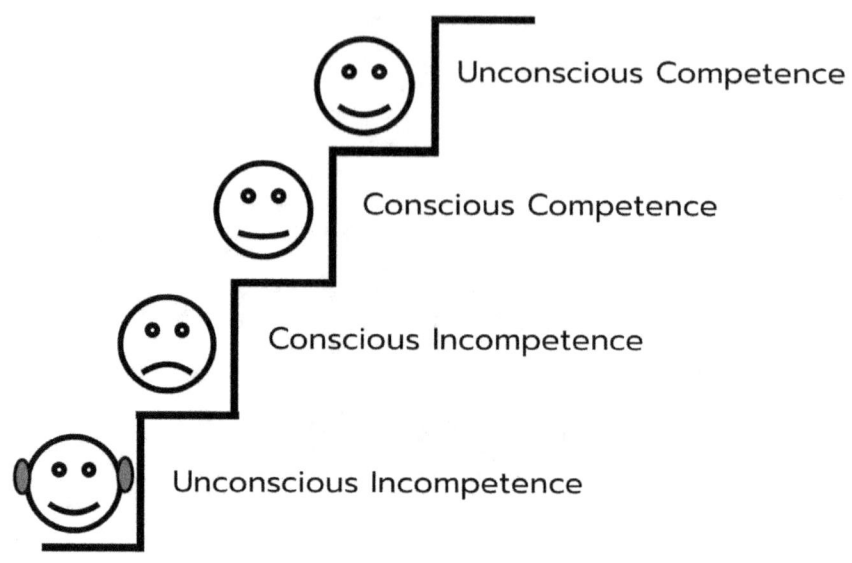

Unconscious Incompetence: Our level of skill has a direct correlation to our level of confidence. Think about it – when something is new to you, it's harder to do, and you don't feel confident about it. But before that stage, there is a stage where we are blissfully ignorant that we are missing this important information – like the teenager crossing the road with his headphones on, we bop along merrily, without a care in the world. At this point, we are incompetent, and we don't even know it!

Conscious competence: Then something happens to let us know we don't know that thing of which we were previously unaware. We are in a position of discomfort, feeling bewildered and often struggling to learn the new information. This is a very uncomfortable space to sit in – we are incompetent, and we know it. And it doesn't feel at all good. At this point we can choose to not worry about it, but we will always know we are incompetent at this thing and often that creates angst; or we can choose to learn and grow.

Conscious competence: Once we have learnt the skills, we take some time to embody our new learning and must constantly concentrate in order to do this new thing well. There is a sense of achievement, but also still a sense of stepping carefully.

Unconscious Competence: At this point we are on autopilot – the task is incredibly simple as we have embodied it completely. We are very comfortable again, quite confident in our ability and may not even remember how difficult it was to learn to start with. In this space, we may be asked to teach someone how to do this thing, and struggle to do so as we may find it hard to remember the steps, as they come so unconsciously.

The example most people resonate with to describe this journey is learning to drive a car. At unconscious incompetence, we are the child in the back seat, unaware of pedals, gears, or indicators, blissfully unaware of why the driver needs to focus on the road, and happy to simply go for a ride.

Then conscious incompetence comes when you get your learner's licence and sit behind the wheel for the first time – a terrifying moment for many. Even applying your foot to the brake can be difficult – which pedal is it and how hard or long do you press?

Conscious competence is that stage when you have passed your test and you are driving alone for the first time – there's nobody to ask if you aren't sure, so you must concentrate hard to remember the rules and the processes. You feel great, but also nervous.

Then, after driving for 20 years, your car somehow finds its own way home – or so it seems. You flick on the indicator at the right moment without even thinking about it, park the car with ease, and drive while holding conversations, singing to music or navigating through unfamiliar territory.

You feel vaguely uneasy when you drive a car you don't usually drive but that passes quickly. The challenge comes when your child comes of age and you have to teach them how to drive, because you say "brake" when what you need to say is "press your left foot on the brake pedal and ease down gently until you feel the car slowing to a stop."

My son is currently learning to drive, and my unconscious competence at driving has led to some conscious incompetence at teaching someone to drive. It's a very daunting space in which to be and a wonderful reminder that when we are training in something new, we must go back to absolute basics.

What Your Body Tells Your Audience

Back in the 70's a chap called Albert Mehrabian performed a whole lot of research into how we convey messages when we speak and how they are perceived by the audience. He is often quoted by speaker trainers as saying that 55 % of audience comprehension comes from body language, 38% from vocal tone and only 7% from the words stated. A closer read indicates to me that Mehrabian was speaking about authenticity.

To be believed these three items must be in sync – The words without the others make someone only 7% believable, vocal on its own only 38% and body language 55% - meaning that body language carries most of the weight when it comes to believability. Mehrabian published his findings in 1981 and communication and leadership trainers around the world took note, training their students on these findings.

Any speaker trainer worth their salt will ensure their students are well versed in how to use the body to effect. The body conveys messages through positioning, stance, posture, facial expressions, eye contact, and movement.

The way in which one walks to the stage, a wobbly stance, wringing or clasped hands, pushing up glasses or running fingers through the hair, hands in the pocket, too many or too few movements, a lack of eye contact, lowered chin and lack of appropriate facial expressions all convey a lack of confidence. No matter how much you know your subject, if you do not manage your body in a manner that looks calm and authoritative, you will miss your mark. This is where the expression "Fake it 'til you make it" originates.

Standing strong, looking the audience in the eye, smiling, moving just enough, and using congruent, natural gestures indicates the speaker is cool and confident, despite what may be going on inside. I always train my students on how to stand strong – that is to have an erect and firm (but not stiff) posture (see previous chapter under shaking or swaying). In every class I have ever trained, this stance has made a big difference to the comfort and confidence of the speakers.

Just as the body position can convey a lack of confidence, going too far in the opposite direction conveys arrogance. One must be careful not to raise their chin about 90 degrees to prevent looking down

The Balloon Principle

the nose at their audience. It is imperative your audience feels you are being respectful. Without respect, you will not gain rapport, and your audience won't like what you have to say, even if they are agree in principle.

Facial expression conveys warmth and animation. The value of a smile cannot be underrated – particularly at the beginning of a presentation when you are just breaking the ice. Smiling is conducive to raising trust – the basis of rapport building. (See STEP 5 – OWNING THE SPACE)

Gestures can work for a variety of reasons – they may add emphasis, describe an item, explain a location or can help in transitioning from one thought to another. The size of the gesture should be relevant to the size of the audience. A small audience would be overwhelmed by large gestures, so arm movement would generally originate from the wrist; a moderately sized audience would benefit from movement originating from the elbows; whilst smaller gestures would be lost on a large audience, so these must originate from the shoulders.

Take care to balance the number of gestures to your presentation. Congruent gestures are key – too many and you look like you are trying to fly or make your own animations; not enough, and you look like a stiff corpse! I always encourage my students to consider if they are a 'stiffy' or a 'flappy' when it comes to arm movements. If they are still, I ask them to deliberately overdo their gestures; if flappy, to try to speak with no gestures. After a while they find the common ground and become more comfortable with the balance of gestures.

Body positioning on the stage can be used to embed or emphasise points subconsciously. You will often see

Acquire Skills

motivational speakers moving to the left for childhood then the right for adulthood or left for pre- and right for post-transition through difficult times. If attempting to use this to effect, the speaker must move so naturally that the audience don't consciously pick up on the movement, as the subconscious embedding is of far greater longevity.

Retaining Engagement

Engagement starts with rapport building. Make sure you give context to your audience at the start – they need to know why what you have to say affects them – the big picture. Then, you need to back that up with some facts, followed by embedding by involving feelings, all while keeping them informed about the process you are following.

If you leave them unsure, they turn off, so explain what is happening and when. Once engaged at the start, your audience will remain engaged if you keep them involved. Speak at them, and they will turn off – speak with them, and you will keep them. Ask questions (especially about them and their needs), facilitate exercises, allow them to discuss and share opinions, tell stories and be open to feedback and questions.

Eye contact is also very important in engagement and often one of the most difficult things to do when you are getting past your initial nervousness. If looking your audience in the eye is too challenging for you, start by looking just above their hairline, then gradually over time, move down to the bridge of the nose. Before you realise it, you will be comfortably looking right into their eyes, engaging them on a much deeper level.

Giving Value

I've been to sales presentations when the speaker gave no value – they told us why we needed what they had then expected us to buy in immediately. Very few people will spend their hard-earned income on signing up to a program if you haven't already shown them that you are capable of what you are offering to teach them. So, demonstrate your value by giving value to your audience, even at a free presentation. They may not be paying with dollars, but they are paying with their time, which is often more valuable to them than money.

Other Skills to Note

There are varying schools of thought about speakers who use notes. In my opinion, notes should be available to use if needed. It is better to look at your notes and regain your place than to stand stammering and lost, or worse still to just come to a stop because you cannot go on.

Personally, I find a motivational or inspirational speaker who uses notes to be lacking in impact. However, an educator or trainer using notes correctly can add impact. Notes can be read on occasion but should not be used as a book – we are public speakers, not public readers! If you are reading your whole presentation it looks like you don't know what you are talking about. When using notes, it is important to continue to maintain eye contact, looking up regularly at your audience.

I tend to use large well-spaced font if I know I am going to need to read, and to use different colours so I can easily define what paragraph I was last looking at in case I lose my place. This allows for maximum audience contact. Also, my notes are usually only on the top 2/3 of the page, so I don't have to look so far down to read – looking down too far can cause your voice to get lost as it doesn't project towards the audience.

When presenting with slides, I use landscape notes with a table format. In the first column, I put the time allowed, in the second a colour print of the slide I am speaking about and the third space has notes for that slide. That way, if I ever need to check my notes, I can quickly find the slide about which I am speaking and move on.

Feedback Is King

There is always another skill to learn, another method to practice. I recommend continual practice in front of an audience who will give you honest and constructive feedback on your presentation. Ask your mentor to work on specific areas where you are aware you need improvement. Make sure they don't try to fix too much all at once – that can become overwhelming. Remember, baby steps are the gentlest way to learn. Either seek a mentor or coach or attend an organisation such as POWERtalk to get this assistance. I still practice regularly and still get pointers on where to improve in my speaking. I am firmly of the belief that one can never know too much.

Reflection

Consider your speaking style - are you a stiffy or a flappy?

How good are you at looking people in the eye?

Can you stand strong?

Where can you get feedback?

Action

Practice overemphasising the opposite movement style to your current one.

Find a book and practice reading out loud to a group, looking up and looking them in the eye regularly.

Practice standing strong whenever you get an opportunity – when getting water from the bubbler, when waiting at the traffic lights to cross the road, when buying coffee. It will become your new norm if you keep practicing.

Find a coach, mentor or group to get honest feedback on your presentation style

Step Three

Liberate Voice

"Think twice before you speak, because your words and influence will plant the seed of either success or failure in the mind of another."
Napoleon Hill

With a 38% weighting on believability, we must also pay attention to our use of vocal tone. Let's start with pitch, pace, pause and projection.

Technique

Our vocal pitch is caused by the rate of vibration of our vocal folds (vocal cords) as air passes through the voice box. The higher the vibration, the higher the pitch. The rate of vibration can be affected by the amount of air we are inhaling, the rate of exhalation, tightness of the surrounding musculature, previous damage or lesions to the vocal cords, and the way in which the mouth and tongue are moving. To hear your vocal pitch variety, try saying "hee, hee, hee, hah, hah, hah, ho, ho, ho". You will notice the "hee" is high and the "Ho" is low. 'Hah" is where your middle range sits.

A voice that is easy to listen to usually stays primarily in middle range, with random variations to both high and low range to add colour. When listening to the intonation of the voice, one must take care not to pop into the high range at the end of each sentence as this can be particularly wearing.

Sitting in the high range for extended periods can make you sound less authoritative, whilst too long in the low range will either be difficult to hear or put your audience to sleep. Generally, women tend to speak in the high range, so need to lower their vocal tone to sound polished, whereas men tend to sit in the lower range and need to raise their tone, which they often find difficult. To assist, I ask the men to speak as though they are speaking to a small child – this helps them find their higher range. At one workshop, I had a man who didn't get what I meant. I asked him if he had a certain way of speaking with his wife when he wanted to get a bit of love. He immediately understood and we all had a good laugh.

The speed at which we speak is of great importance. These days most people are rushing. The consequence is we often speak too quickly, and important information is missed. When you are offering information in a longer package (ie speaking publicly) this is even more problematic. It's important to allow your listener time to catch up with what you are saying, for important concepts to be understood. Remember, your audience doesn't have the benefit of written word, which allows them to review when they missed something. Take the time for them to understand and keep up with your information.

For those with an accent – or those listening who usually speak a different language – slowing the pace is of even greater importance. Time must be allowed for translation, and to work out what the word was when it was pronounced differently to the way they are used to hearing it.

Meditation and grounding, or simply taking some space to relax prior to speaking can help to slow down your pace, so your audience can understand better. Another way of slowing down is an exercise that interrupts your brain patterns. Take any sentence and read it out loud in full. Then insert a multi-syllable word in between each word of the sentence, reading it out loud eg. "Elephant ear" could be inserted between each word. Then after reading aloud with the interrupter between each word, read the sentence out loud again. You will note each word is enunciated more clearly when you speak a little more slowly. This is also a good exercise to practice if you are a person who trips over their words or gets tongue-tied when speaking.

Care not to go too slow must also be taken. Very slow speech can lose the audience as they get bored or lose track of what you are talking about. Variety of pace adds light and shade to the story you are telling. Fast speech suggests enthusiasm or danger, slow can be sexy or gentle.

Pause is one of the greatest vocal tools. A speech that is too fast can be rescued by regular pauses, allowing the audience to catch up. Pause adds enormous impact to your speech – allowing for extra emphasis on words or sections of the speech. Pause, however, is one of the most difficult things to get used to doing when standing in front of a group. Master the art of standing still and silent in front of an audience, and your credibility as a speaker will rapidly raise skywards.

When practicing pause, take a red (or other bright coloured) pen and mark vertical lines between words where you wish to make a pause. Use two lines for a longer pause and three for a very long pause. Practice reading and doing a mental count between the words where the pauses have been marked. It takes a while before it becomes automatic, but you will get there.

Of course, none of this is of any use if the audience cannot hear what you are saying. Projection is the term for allowing your voice to be pushed across the room, so it reaches all your audience. Some people have natural projection (think big, booming voice) while others barely squeak. To improve projection, there are several contributing factors. Firstly, it is important to clarify that projection and yelling are not the same. If you yell to get your voice across a room, it will be a matter of time before you damage your voice – sometimes permanently.

Secondly, do your best to improve your lung capacity. A big booming voice is created through resonance and most of that happens in the upper chest area. The voice vibrates in the chest and consequently comes out a whole lot louder. Also, the lower abdominal muscles can be used to create a base for your voice by allowing pressure to be held within the abdomen which supports the upper body. Add to that a lower tone, a relaxed throat and facial muscles, and an adequately open mouth with the breath being directed towards the audience, and your voice will be much stronger. Until you have mastered this, you might consider using a microphone to assist.

Before speaking, I recommend vocal warmup exercises. There are several available. Enunciation exercises will loosen the tongue and prevent tongue-ties. Lip bubbling and yawning loosen the muscles of the face and throat and allow for better tonality. Siren-ing warms up your tonality and allows for ease of movement between registers.

Substance

Have you ever watched a politician answering a media question and counted the number of times they say "um" and "er"? Some are worse than others – the late Bob Hawke was a cracker! I remember counting over 30 ums one night in about one minute. Eventually, you only hear the ums, and the message is missed.

Those of us who do speaker training call these filler words. They come about because we have been conditioned to hold the floor in a conversation by filling in the spaces with "um" or "er", so nobody else takes over the conversation. But when we are speaking at the front of a room, that is no longer an issue, and the words can become distracting and unattractive.

To remove filler words, start to pay attention to them. When you recognise you are about to "um" or "er", take a breath instead and simply pause. It will feel strange to start with (remember, we are now consciously incompetent in this space) but that will soon pass, and you will become unconsciously competent at leaving the fillers out.

The other thing that will help you leave out fillers and speak more directly is being sure of who you are and what you are about. When you aren't afraid to be seen, you will be less afraid to be heard. The follow-on effect on your confidence and your ability to comfortably and calmly speak to your audience without needing to hesitate, becomes obvious. You become a leader of substance.

Relevance

You may have heard people say, 'it's all about the audience' and that is absolutely true. If what you have to say is of no relevance to your audience, they will not listen. Just as the message must be relevant to the audience, the vocals must also be relevant to the words being spoken. This is what Mehrabian was on about with his studies. If you need convincing, try saying," I hate you" in a light and joking tone – or "I love you" in a dark and sinister one. The tonality is misaligned with the words and changes the meaning. This can be used to great effect when adding humour to a speech.

Now you have the body language and the vocal tone sorted, let's move on to the words of your presentation, and how to let them flow.

Reflection

Where does your voice naturally sit?

Do you use up-swings at the end of sentences?

Do you speak quickly, or slowly?

Do you project your voice and enunciate clearly?

Action

Record yourself speaking and listen for the areas to work on.

Practice reading passages with 'elephant ear' or 'green gorilla' or any other multi-syllable phrase between the words to slow your speech down.

Practice projecting your voice clearly across a room without yelling.

Look up some vocal warmup exercises you can use to raise or lower your tone as required.

Start to become aware of filler words and their use by counting "ums" and "ers" when hearing people speak (you'll hate me for this later!) then practice leaving filler words out when speaking with friends.

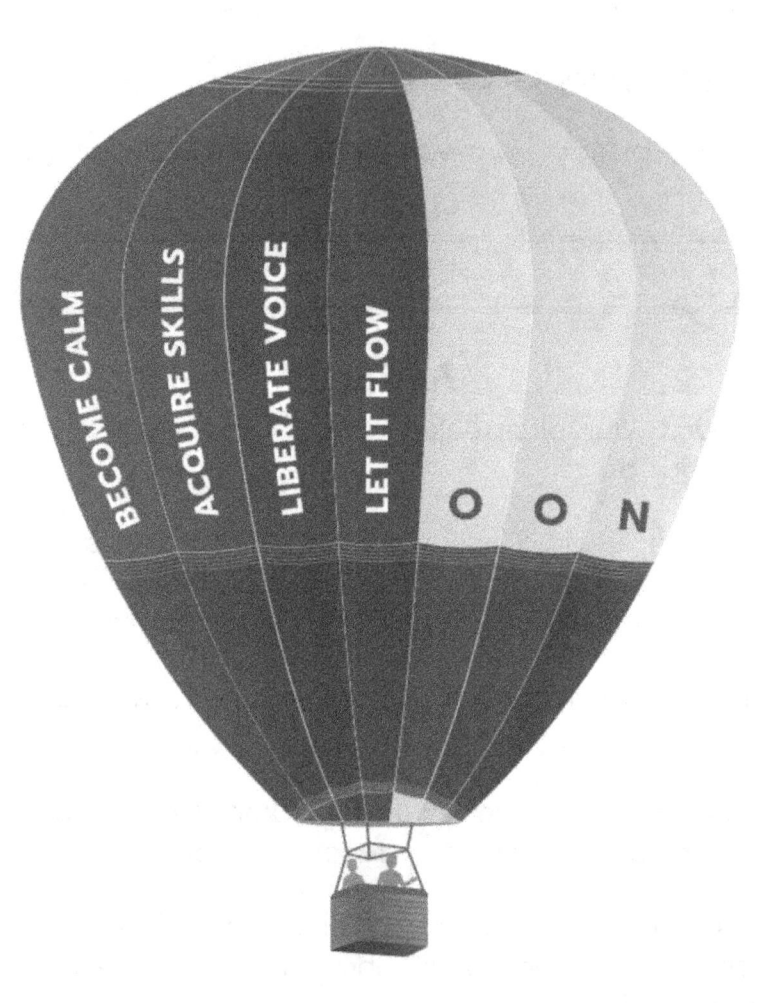

Step Four
Let It Flow

"What you really want for yourself is always trying to break through, just as a cooling breeze flows through an open window on a hot day. Your part is to open the windows of your mind."
Vernon Howard

The concept of flow is one I find both fascinating and liberating. For the first 40+ years of my life, I lived a journey of control. As a child, I was closely controlled by my parents who didn't know any different having lived the same journey. And considering they had 6 children in 8 years, life would quite likely have been complete chaos without it. The downside was that we didn't learn how to control ourselves, only how to control others.

As an adult the pattern continued. I desperately tried to control everything and everyone around me but had little self-control. I looked for someone to control me, and my poor husband was regularly blamed for my shortcomings. This made for a journey of constant struggle. I was unhappy in life, in business, and in my marriage.

After the birth of my second child who was conceived using IVF (what an uncontrollable journey that was!) I spiralled into a deep depression. I knew something was very wrong – I had no energy, no joie de vivre. I felt like I was on autopilot, pushing myself every day to continue. I wanted my children so very much but didn't have the energy to love them in the way I wanted to.

I couldn't understand – I had everything I ever wanted but was so disengaged from life, that I wanted out. Then one very dark moment, I had a thought so incomprehensible that it sent me rushing for help. And that very dark moment became the turning point for me, from which I began to learn how letting go of the desperate need to control everything brought balance and energy with it.

Therapy was followed by training in Counselling and Business and then Leadership, coaching and mentoring. I took every opportunity to learn about who I was, and how to accept every facet of myself. I learnt about thinking patterns, personality types, Emotional Intelligence, Crucial conversation skills, conversational intelligence and much more.

The overarching lesson I took away was of acceptance – acceptance of others and their actions; or diversity; myself and all that I was; of emotions and their role; and most importantly of how allowing things to just be, in flow, held a magnificent power.

When all things can be as they were intended, when emotions serve a purpose and are not there to be avoided, and when judgement and control are released, life becomes simple and filled with ease. That is where the greatest magic happens, because in that space, you can allow yourself to truly **be** yourself and you become open to the lessons of the universe.

The root cause of my depression was that I had been holding back and not being myself. I had judged myself harshly and not accepted the gifts I had been given. It ate away at me until I was almost completely gone. The road back was long, but the destination now is much more exciting, inspiring and easy than I ever dreamed possible. I encourage anyone feeling that they cannot live in flow or be themselves to seek help so that they can get into flow. The peace you will find there is remarkable.

So, what has flow got to do with speaking?

A couple of things. Firstly, let's look at flow as related to the journey. My advice is don't try to force it. There is a season for all things, and life happens in its own time. That doesn't mean, sit back and wait for it to happen, without any effort. What it means is that if you put all things in place, if you have a clear vision and mission, are trained in and practiced in your craft, employ working strategies and keep the faith, it will come in its own time.

It's common for people who want to make a difference to feel it needed to happen yesterday — to get frustrated and give up when it takes too long or gets too hard. But difficulty is what makes us stronger — if you really want what you say you want, hold the vision close. If you have let go of something you really believe is part of your journey, take it up again. Sometimes the break is all part of the grand plan in which we live.

For some, clarifying the vision is the issue, which makes for more difficulty. The journey through difficult times often holds keys to our mission. When we refuse to embrace ourselves and our innermost desires, we are holding back from living our purpose.

When you are truly yourself and living congruently with your values and beliefs, your vision and mission will become very clear. Once that happens, it is time to share it.

Now, let's look at flow related to the format of a presentation. To share your message in a manner that is heard, understood and acted upon, it must be structured in a format that flows and is easy to listen to and encourages action. If your format does not flow, the message may not get through, so structure is very important. Without a call to act, your presentation may not achieve its desired outcome.

Here are some basic structure pointers to help.

Suggestions to Note

No matter when you speak, you must always do so with an anticipated outcome. Speaking with no intention of an outcome is like sailing without a destination – you will get lost. Start with the end in mind. Decide the outcome you want from sharing the information you are sharing. Note that outcome and then decide how you will achieve it. Create a thesis and a theme to run through your presentation. Brainstorm ideas to support your thesis, then decide between using three or five main points that best support your thesis and lead to your outcome. Now, find some evidence to back up your argument, and create your speech body, connecting each point to the following point so the speech has flow. Then add an attention-catching introduction and an activating conclusion that makes your audience take the action you have suggested.

Introductions

The most crucial moments of any speech or presentation are the first five minutes. And of those five minutes, the first one minute is key. Not only is the way you approach the stage or lectern important (see STEP 5 - OWN THE SPACE) but the opening statements are also vital. Your words and actions need to grab the attention of the audience, engaging their emotional buy-in to what you are saying. You can do this in several ways, including the use of any of the following:

- An anecdote – an anecdote (not an antidote as it is often mispronounced) is a short story about a person or incident, not necessarily all truth. Remember if you use humour, at this point it needs to be self-deprecating, not aimed at your audience. Unless you are a practiced comedian, avoid the use of jokes at the start of a presentation as it can go very flat. Remember, this is the part of the presentation when they are still getting to know you.
- A scenario – this usually starts with "imagine this" and paints a picture in the mind of the audience
- A quote – there are so many to choose from and so many ways to use them. You must always reference the person whose words you are using and if you are a regular quote

user, try to mix up the way you introduce who said it.
- A declarative statement – this is a strong statement of belief. It may be something that really resonates with your audience, or something that really challenges them to get them listening to you and reacting to what you are saying. If you are challenging them, have your arguments ready to persuade them to keep listening.
- A rhetorical question – a question to which you do not expect an answer. Even so, make sure you leave a pause after it, so that the audience has time to mull over what their opinion is of the answer to the question.
- An actual question – if using a question to which you anticipate an answer, be prepared to facilitate the response – you might ask them to raise their hand if they agree or suggest a specific person to answer. If you do not facilitate, you may lose control of the room which is not a good start.
- A short poem – this needs to be a very engaging and simple poem, or a few lines from a poem. Too long and your audience will disengage. Poems can be used very effectively by reading more of the introduction's poem in the conclusion.

When you start, your first words need to engage your audience. They are here to listen – give them something attention grabbing to listen to. If you want to ask them how they are, save it for a few moments in. The most effective openings will use 10 – 15 seconds of attention-grabbing material, followed by a greeting to the audience, not the other way around.

Conclusions

Conclusions should wind up your speech or presentation and point directly to the required outcome of the speech. If your outcome was to educate, your conclusion will repeat the main points you wish your audience to remember. If to inspire, you might repeat your thesis and add some words to suggest the next step towards reaching that pinnacle to which you have been asking your audience to aspire. If to persuade or sell, a clear call to action is required – this must very clearly direct your audience as to what to do to sign up, or follow, or embody your cause.

Conclusions should refer in some way to the introduction in order to neatly wrap up the presentation and to leave your audience realising that the end has been reached. Always try to leave on a high note – regardless of how dark the content of you talk might have been. If you leave your audience feeling there is no hope, they will not enlist to help out.

Memory

There are three significant factors to your audience remembering what you have told them. They will more easily remember the first or last thing you told them; the things you repeated; or the things that left them with a sense of urgency due to a deep connection to their values and beliefs.

Therefore, structure is important. Consider the order in which you plan to deliver the information. If your most important point is buried in the middle, your audience will miss it. That doesn't mean fill the middle with fluff – you will lose their attention if you do. The middle section will require values alignment or repetition, so it is more memorable.

Rule of Three

Another secret to memory is that our human brain is wired to recognise certain patterns. Some suggest the wiring is from learned patterns introduced throughout our lives, others say it is a left-brain, right-brain thing. It doesn't really matter where it comes from. What matters is that it works! The rule of three says that the simplest pattern to remember is a three – such as 1, 2, 3; or A, B, C; or red, white and blue; Tom, Dick and Harry... the combinations are endless.

If you want your audience to have a takeaway message they remember, working in threes will take you a long way towards that end.

To make a speech structure that works using this rule, you can have an introduction that grabs their attention, a body with three main points and a conclusion. I always recommend that conclusion is reflective of the introduction in some way, so the whole speech is tied up nicely in a package.

Odds and Rounds

Just as we like threes, our next favourite numbers are 5, 7 or 10. This comes in handy when there is too much information to handle in just three points. I don't recommend more than 7 (unless it is quite long, and then you could do 10) as it is difficult to remember a list of more than seven items. Even that gets a bit tricky!

Fish

A couple of years ago, I was asked to train a group of homeless people in speaking so they could speak for a Not-for-profit organisation at corporate fundraising events. Some of these people were marginalised with mental health issues or were illiterate so had memory issues and could not take or read notes. I had to create a simple structure that they could use for shorter speeches or longer speeches (anything from a couple of minutes to an hour) to remember the parts of their speech without needing to read. I came up with a visual model of a fish. I have shared this model many times since, and every time it has been received as a brilliant tool.

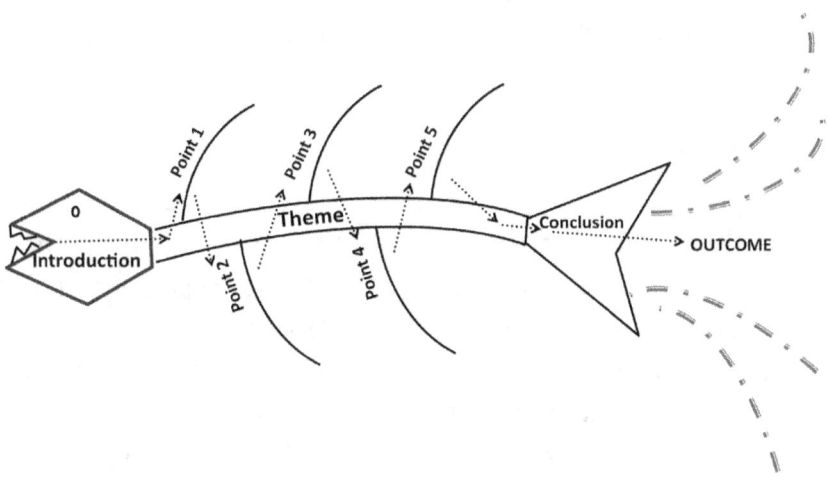

The elements of the fish are as follows. The head is the introduction – it has teeth to grab the audience's attention. The spine is the theme and joins the introduction to the conclusion. The tail is the conclusion. It is shaped vaguely similarly to the head to remind the speaker to reflect on their introductory remarks during the conclusion. In its wake is the outcome – the fish must move in a way that creates the outcome you want. The bones – either 3 or 5 or occasionally 7 are on alternating sides of the spine. The speech flows along from the head through the theme to the first spine (point) through the theme again to the second spine and so on until it reaches the tail where it concludes leaving the outcome as desired.

When the speech is short, you only share the bare bones – a simple introduction, a mention of the spines (points) joined by the theme and a short call to action in the tail. When it is a longer speech, you add flesh to the bones, and give more information on each point, before passing through the theme to the next point. You may choose to use rule of three to add flesh to the bones. This format can even be used for a course with each spine being a module. It is a very versatile and useful model to use and easy to remember.

Potency

Now that you have your structure and can piece together your presentation, it's time to ramp it up another step so it has the power and impact you want it to have by reaching your entire audience. There is an assumption that you will never have the attention of everyone in the room. I beg to differ. If you structure and present in a manner that flows and speaks to everyone in the room, there is no reason why you wouldn't have their attention.

The best and simplest way to achieve this is to align with the thinking patterns and preferences of your audience.

As a certified HBDI ® Practitioner, I regularly debrief profiles for individuals and teams to assist them with communication through an understanding of their personal thinking preferences and the preferences of others in their team or circle.

Let It Flow

The HBDI ® (Herrmann Brain Dominance Instrument) profiling tool as developed by Ned Herrmann, who recognised back in the 1960's that there were some vast differences between the thinking style preference of individuals. He created the tool after a great deal of research, and it has been successfully applied innumerable times throughout the world in business and personal environments. Briefly, the tool illustrates the brain and thinking preferences in quadrants as follows:

A or blue quadrant - upper left – a preference for data, analysis, technical information – these people need to hear the bare facts without fluff.

B or green quadrant - lower left – a preference for organisation and processes, concern with safety and planning; they love the details – these people need structure and to be told what is coming and when to expect it; if you ramble, you lose them.

C or red quadrant - lower right – emotionally driven and nurturing – these people need to know everyone is ok with what is being shared, they need the emotional response to truly embed their learning.

D or yellow quadrant - upper right – creative thinkers, problem solvers, integrators and synthesisers - these are big picture people and happy to fly by the seat of their pants, provided they have and understand the context of what you are talking about and how it fits into the big picture. They can follow a ramble and connect the dots.

The tool recognises that all quadrants are of equal value, so there is no wrong or right quadrant. There are consequences of your thinking preference – if you strongly prefer a certain preference, your behaviour and the way you communicate will be affected by that preference. Issues may arise when communicating with people who have strong preferences for differing styles. When your rating is particularly low in a quadrant, it is likely you will not consider communicating in a style that suits those audience members who are strong in that quadrant. Hence, understanding how to present from each quadrant and including all quadrants in your presentation will help you reach every individual audience member. Unless you have a profile of every person in the room, the recommendation is to go for a whole brain approach – that is, speak from all four quadrants in your presentation.

The recommended order for doing this is to start with context – "why you need to hear what I am saying" – once you have done this the yellow people will stay with you right through.

Then, go to the supporting data and statistics. Blues will cope with you giving context, but they'll turn off if you go anywhere else before you give them a reason to believe you by telling them the facts and figures that back up your research.

Follow that with the emotional impact for the red quadrant – reassure the audience that they are in a safe space and make sure everyone is coping what you have told them so far. Allow space to share their feelings and use emotive language throughout the presentation to activate their emotional response.

Don't forget the green quadrant – "The aim of the presentation is; what we will do is...; this is what we are going to do first, then that, then this and we'll finish with this; your expected outcome will be that; and we'll also cover what to do if..." In this section, include instructions on behaviour, question time, facilities and emergency procedures.

This formula will serve you if you use it in your introduction and throughout your presentation, as it addresses the needs of every person in the room's thinking preference.

The only time to deviate from this formula is if you are sharing or debriefing a particularly emotional situation. Highly charged emotional content must be handled very carefully – the emotional well-being of your audience must be considered. As a speaker, you are a leader. As a leader, you have a responsibility for the well-being of those you are leading. Be aware of potential triggers, and of ensuring there are processes in place to support anyone in your audience who may become triggered. Throughout the presentation, check in regularly with the group. A large percentage of any audience has not learned to embrace all emotions and will disengage if things become too emotionally challenging. To prevent or mitigate disengagement or triggering in these situations, share context, then give emotional support before following the remainder of the formula, then again check in to see that all are feeling supported emotionally (i.e. Yellow, red, blue, red, green, red).

Feelings

In Maya Angelou's words, "...People will forget what you said, People will forget what you did. People will never forget how you made them feel."

A speaker who speaks from the heart has far more impact than one who is simply sharing information

– oftentimes referred to as speaking from the head. But, just as the right balance of movement or vocal variation is required, so is the right balance of emotion. Emotions and your use of them can make or break your presentation. I've already mentioned the effect too much emotion can have on an audience. When there is not enough emotion, you will become easily forgettable and have little impact. This is particularly important when you are selling a product, service or concept.

When selling, you are asking your buyer to make a change – they are changing their circumstances, their finances, their future. Humans are naturally resistant to change. The Beckhard-Harris model for Change states that in order to reduce resistance to change, there must be dissatisfaction with the status quo, a clear vision for change and knowledge of the first step to take. Hence, your audience must feel the pain of the problem and be allowed to sit in that space long enough to want the solution you are offering. In addition, you must advise them of your vision or product to solve that pain and of the first steps to take in order to acquire that product or become a supporter of your vision.

Story

Since the beginning of time, humans have used story for learning and sharing of wisdom. Most people know that stories help your audience remember you and what you have offered them. But they do so much more than that. Stories help your audience get to know you on a deeper level. In a story you can show your values and beliefs, knowledge and expertise while building connections by touching on common interests or experiences. Those connections are deepened by creating emotional alignments through allowing your audience to see your vulnerabilities and the parts of your journey that are relevant to them and their needs.

Your words must draw a picture and elicit a response. Emotive words are key – look for stronger words to use when you are trying to make a point reach deeper. Some examples would be describing feeling upset as feeling shattered or devastated; a bad smell as putrid or rancid in place of offensive; still on the smell thread, it could assail your nostrils, not reach them; or when describing people who are poor, words such as destitute, impoverished, beggarly or poverty-stricken could be used.

Description involving the senses will also help to engage more of the audience – often people have a preference of sense, such as auditory, visual, or kinaesthetic (or tactile). Make sure you include word pictures, as well as what sounds, smells or tastes are included as well as how it made you (or those around you) feel.

Through storytelling you can build trust, make the invisible visible and help your audience discover a world in which they want to participate.

Story can also be used to support your claims – sharing a story of change can be a very inspiring and persuasive tool. Story must be combined with emotion for it to be effective - without emotion story becomes simple facts and doesn't feel real to the listener. Without that sense of real-ness or honesty, your story will disengage and lose your potential follower. Another way to lose someone through story is sharing things that have no relevance to the listener. This can be perceived as ego indulgence or as time wasting, both of which will not serve you.

My seven 'be' keys for storytelling are:

1. Be real – don't try to be anyone but you. An inauthentic story will have no or negative impact.
2. Be relevant – you don't have to tell everything that has ever happened. Share what is relevant to your audience and to the desired outcome.
3. Be honest – don't make stuff up just to make a point – you will get caught out and lose trust
4. Be open – show the real you – your thoughts, values, beliefs, aspirations, mission and vision. That way you will find your tribe of extraordinary people.
5. Be vulnerable – let them see your emotions and elicit an emotional response. Remember a tear will not undermine you (see crying under STEP 1 – BECOME CALM)
6. Be in service – when you share to serve, you will gain more attention, more buy-in, and more impact.
7. Be a guide – remember to advise your audience what to do next to move them to action.

Structure your presentation in an easy-to-follow coherent dialogue, combining story and emotion, and do so with flow and your presentation will be extraordinarily potent.

Reflection

What is the outcome you want from sharing the information you are sharing?

What are the main points you will use to support that information?

How can you introduce the subject in a way that will grab your audience's attention?

How will you complete your presentation?

What action do you want them to take as a result of your presentation?

Action

Start with the end in mind.

On a board or paper, note the desired outcome and then decide how you will achieve it. Define your thesis and theme. Decide what points you will use and what stories you can include.

Revise and check that what you have chosen will serve the desired outcome. Adjust if necessary.

Write a rough draft of the body of the presentation. Insert stories, then find emotive words to replace simple one. Check you have spoken to the senses.

Create a call to action that guides your audience on what action to take next. Then, create your introduction and conclusion.

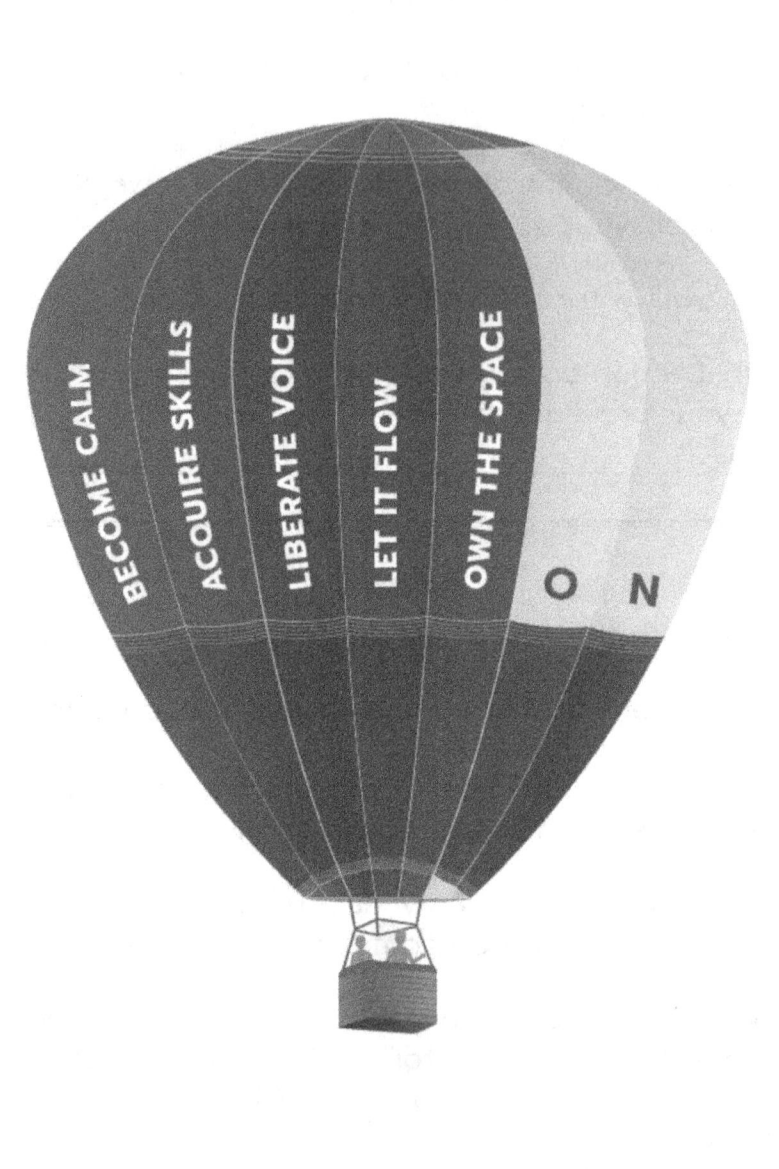

Step Five
Own the Space

If you want to become a world-class speaker, this chapter is possibly the most important of this book. It contains the step that holds the secret between a good speaker and an outstanding one. I struggled with this for a very long time – my past, my thoughts, and the people surrounding me were all obstructing my trajectory. But the biggest issue was my inability to lead myself – to own my actions, my thoughts, my feelings, my personal space and just be me. Because I didn't know who I was, I couldn't work out my purpose, and that left me aimless, a ship without a rudder, powerless to create an impact, and lost in the sea of speakers on the market.

Finding purpose is a huge issue for many people. We get frustrated, run around trying a million different things, reading self-help books, listening to gurus, consulting psychics and trying just about anything to find our why; all the while keeping ever so busy and trying to look like we have everything under control. These actions often don't help – in fact, it's a soul-destroying space to be in! We are afraid to let anyone see the real us, to be open and vulnerable, or to let people know we are struggling with anything, because as a leader, we feel we should know it all.

In actuality, the best leaders actively and regularly admit to not knowing it all. In addition, a deep curiosity and open-ness to learning drives them towards greatness.

"But", I hear you say, "I'm not trying to be a leader, I just want to speak comfortably."

When you hold the floor in front of a group, you are in a leadership position. Attention to your words, body language and vocals will help add potency to your presentation, but you will come undone if you are unable to hold the space with sincere authenticity and embody leadership. You must walk the talk of your message and vision and that doesn't stop when you're not in front of a group speaking to them – it's an all-in, 24/7 thing! So, where do you start?

Stop

You start by being still. By taking the time to get to really know yourself. I recommend meditation – for the special something you are looking for will be found within you. Be still and quiet. Reflect on who you are, what you truly believe and value, what makes you special, why you are the person to do this thing you have been called to do. When you come to the realisation that you have something nobody else has, your ability to own the space as a leader will shine.

Poise

Owning the space requires you to look the part. Looks are not only about hair, makeup and style of dress – although they are part of it. Looks include the way in which you walk and talk, the way in which you listen, the way you hold your body, when standing or sitting. Imagine you are at an event awaiting the speaker. The compere introduces them, and they saunter out, head down, hair akimbo, dressed in a dirty oversized t-shirt and ripped jeans with bare feet. Your first impression is not great!

Just as a speaker needs to start their presentation with care to engage their speakers, they need to arrive in a manner that has the audience looking for the right reasons, and without harsh judgement. The trust level of the audience drops when the speaker looks unmotivated.

Apart from looking the part, the right clothes can make a huge difference to your confidence level. From my late 20's, I spent 15 years in the fashion industry as a couturiere. I designed and made bridal and special occasion wear and often, it was those whose body shape wasn't the perfect model size (that's most of us) who would come to have their gowns specially made because the off-the-shelf items didn't look good on them. Often, these people were down on themselves and felt unattractive due to their shape or size. When a garment was made specially for them, styled perfectly for their shape, and fitting well, the effect on them was immediately visible. They would put the piece on and walk to the mirror, and when they saw themselves, would light up! They'd go from shoulders down to standing tall, radiating confidence and happiness. If you are down on yourself, I recommend finding that one outfit that makes you look and feel smashing –

your confidence will soar and when you are feeling confident, anything feels possible. You can't put a price on that!

Your approach to the lectern – or to the front of the room – should exude confidence and enthusiasm. That doesn't mean you must jump around and dance (although feel free to do that if it is your style). Your walk should be direct and purposeful, head held straight, a warm smile as you look around and immediately making connections with the audience. You should always acknowledge the compere – even if it is a nonverbal acknowledgement such as a handshake or hug. That immediately shows you as being respectful and creates a positive perception within the room.

When you arrive, pause and smile before starting to speak. This allows your audience to do what we all do (but try to pretend we don't) – to look you up and down. If you start to speak immediately, you lose impact as they aren't paying full attention yet. Allow them a silent count of three, give your opening statement, then greet them by starting with a collective description (e.g. ladies and gentlemen; beautiful souls; amazing life engineers; or anything else that fits) followed by an appropriate salutation (e.g. Good morning; hi there; welcome). Pause again then commence your presentation. Structuring the greeting like this creates an opportunity for audience response, immediately engaging them and bringing their focus to you.

Throughout your presentation, use a strong stance and try not to sway or pace, as each of these are distracting and convey a sense of nervousness.

Be open to your audience's responses – learn to read their body language to ascertain if you are getting through or if they are getting tired and need a break or a laugh to re-energise. Modify your presentation if required to ensure your audience understands concepts and you have buy-in from them. Know your subject matter. Be prepared to answer questions and learn how to do this comfortably and authoritatively. If you don't know an answer, don't pretend you do – I can assure there is quite likely someone in the room who does, and you will lose your credibility if you fudge an answer. Nobody can ever possibly know all there is to know about a subject, so don't be afraid to be honest about not knowing. You may choose to throw the answer to the group, brainstorm an answer or offer to do some research and get back to them with the answer.

Sincerity

Sincerity is a trust-based entity. When you fail to deliver, you break trust so if you offer to get back to someone during a presentation, make sure you do.

Building trust is key to establishing rapport and getting buy-in from your audience, but it doesn't start with the presentation. It goes as far back as your marketing and branding. You must present yourself as trustworthy – again this goes back to walking your talk. If you live out of alignment with your message, you become untrustworthy.

On the day of your presentation, meet as many of the attendees as you can prior to speaking and form a relationship with them. Get to know who they are – what makes them tick, what lights them up. In a pre-presentation conversation, you can also get indications of the thinking preferences of various audience members. When presenting and seeing someone seems confused, having an idea of their preference assists you to guide them to understand far more quickly.

Building trust is a difficult concept for many people. Social anxiety is rife in our world of digital connection, where many are no longer comfortable with face-to-face communication. Many of my workshop attendees find it liberating to discover that our brains are wired to create connections – we are motivated to look for things to LIKE about people when we meet them.

Neuroscience explains that in the same area as what is regarded as the third eye, we have an area named the Rostro Medial Prefrontal Cortex (RMPFC) which is responsible for finding similarities to use as a basis for connection. Our bodies have a trust-distrust hormone balance. The trust hormone is Oxytocin and distrust hormone is Cortisol. These hormones co-regulate – meaning that if one goes up, the other goes down. If the RMPFC finds no similarities, distrust rises and with it, up goes the cortisol level. If the similarities are found, Oxytocin rises and like and trust is formed. The interesting part is that the RMPFC can also detect the trust-distrust level of those who surround you and regulate your level in accordance with theirs. Meaning if their oxytocin is high, yours will go up creating a like and trust scenario; or if their cortisone is high, yours will also elevate, raising your level of distrust. This explains why sometimes, your 'spider-senses' tingle when you meet someone, and you immediately like them – or dislike them! Just as you have these senses and abilities, so does your audience. Meaning you can influence how they feel about you just by sincerely radiating love in their direction. Meditation is great preparation for speakers as it allows them to get into the peaceful state that radiates trust and love;

thus, assisting to speed up the trust-building process. Furthermore, if you consider your presentation content as something special, you are giving them a gift. Everybody loves a gift, so reframing your thoughts to that understanding will also help to activate the Oxytocin levels and increase trust.

Charisma

Charismatic speakers move an audience to action – they get them to follow and participate in their vision.

Charisma also requires trust, but you can trust someone without finding yourself wanting to follow them and do their will. So, what is it that draws people to someone and makes them followers?

Charisma or charm comes from a combination of several factors, not the least being relatability. You must be real enough that people can relate to who you are – not aloof and removed from the everyday activities of average people.

A large factor in Charisma is an attitude of acceptance and nonjudgement. If a leader shows that they respect all people and their way of life that leader becomes far more popular and likely to gather followers – they are more likeable. Along with respect, the leader must show interest in the wellbeing of the people whom they are leading. They can do this by being fully present in any interaction – this includes not being distracted by screens, phones, books, notes etc. Paying full attention shows the other parties that you hold them in high regard and offers them an opportunity to present points of view that can assist your cause, thereby being mutually beneficial.

There are times in life where despite our best efforts, things go wrong. In those moments, we are best served through applying emotional intelligence (EI). Through embodying EI, we embrace emotion by finding the lessons in every emotion we feel. We own the emotional response and manage the emotion, not allowing it to control us and not taking out our frustrations on those around us. If we feel frustrated, we look at the lesson in the situation... What is it exactly that makes us feel that way? Understanding the root cause of the situation and applying strategies to alleviate it, allows us to weather whatever emotional moments life may throw at us. Becoming less reactive is the first step. The next step is to apply strategies to prevent the same issues arising again – to be proactive.

Excellence in communication, being open and honest about our challenges, listening to connect, allowing for involvement of others and both giving and receiving encouragement, support and mentoring all add to the package. The leader must be able to be persuasive, in a manner that allows the follower to feel valued and respected for the action they have taken, not coerced into taking that action.

The leader must also recognise when to step away. We can manage our own responses to situations, and we can assist others who allow us to, but we don't get to manage everyone's responses all the time. There are times when allowing space for people to settle or come back to calm is required. Sometimes, planting a seed, then stepping away and allowing time for that seed to germinate in the mind of our audience is the most appropriate course of action. As a leader we must recognise and respect individual processing timeframes and allow them the space to think. Having said that, we must also try to stay within specified timeframes. Being careless with time can disengage an audience and destroy mutual respect.

Probably one of the biggest factors in charisma is the knowledge of self. Knowing what matters most to you, your values, and your beliefs and being able to stand strong in the knowledge that while this thing you are passionate about may not matter to everyone, it matters to you, and you are prepared to live true to those values and beliefs and be yourself. Respecting the non-believers whilst not giving up, being resilient and being yourself, fully wholly, and unapologetically gives you a sense of presence in all that you do. Being aware of your shortcomings and working in strength while growing in the areas of challenge makes you a person who will be admired and appreciated.

To that end, clarity of vision (where you want this to go) and a compelling mission (how you will get there) and being able to enlist others to come along for the ride are pivotal. If you don't know what you stand for, you cannot communicate it to others and until you can communicate your vision and mission, you will struggle to find the supporters you require.

Reflection

What is your vision (the change you want to see in the world)?

What is your mission (the way in which you intend to achieve that change)?

Who can you encourage to join you in the mission?

What are your values and beliefs and how will they impact on the mission and vision?

Action

List your values and beliefs and look for aligned people who share about the same issues. Check to see if anyone else is already doing what you decide to do and consider if you could collaborate or enter a joint venture with them – it's much easier to work as a team than to split resources.

Consider what emotions create chaos for you. Examine the lesson behind the emotion and apply proactive strategies to assist in future episodes. Be kind to yourself when you slip up – we are all human and we all get it wrong sometimes.

Consider what kinds of programmes and workshops you could run to get your message out and to encourage and support people to work with you towards your goal.

BECOME CALM · ACQUIRE SKILLS · LIBERATE VOICE · LET IT FLOW · OWN THE SPACE · OPERATE DEVICES

Step Six

Operate Devices

To be a professional speaker, one needs to be able to seamlessly operate the physical tools of the trade. If you are constantly calling for assistance when setting up or during your talk, your credibility will drop. Things can, and often do, go wrong with audio-visual devices, so it is imperative that you are able to deal with those moments when they arise.

Audio

Vocal projection will get your though in a small room, but a larger space will require audio assistance. When people think of speakers and audio devices, their mind will generally go to microphone usage which we will discuss shortly, but microphones are not the only audio device a speaker might use. A basic understanding of troubleshooting for music players, and computer audio is also necessary. If you plan to use these, make sure you are familiar with the device you plan to use and practice outside of the environment. Also, allow sound-check time when doing set-up. Room acoustics vary. What seems enough in one room may be completely insufficient (or overwhelming) in another. If you plan to use music for thinking time when running workshops, bear in mind some of your audience may find it distracting and may require the option of moving to another space to work in quiet.

Microphones

Using a microphone can be a challenge when you first start. It can be a bit of a shock to hear your voice amplified and projected across a room. When we speak without a microphone, we hear our voice internally through our facial bones. When it is amplified, we are hearing it played back from outside of us and that can sound quite different to what we are used to hearing. Bear with it – you will get used to it.

There are many different types and styles of microphones. Microphones work by receiving sound waves and carrying them to an amplifier to make them louder. Reception of waves may be from one direction (unidirectional or directional) or all directions (multi-directional or omni-directional). Unidirectional microphones decrease the amount of outside noise picked up by the microphone, so can give a much clearer sound. The downside it that if you are not speaking in the direction of the receiver, your sound can drop out or be muffled. When holding a unidirectional microphone, one must be very careful to ensure the voice is directed into the top of the microphone, with the instrument angled in such a way as to not obstruct the view of the speaker's face.

Operate Devices

The three main microphone styles for speaking are hand-held, lavaliere or headset microphones. Each have their advantages and disadvantages. A reasonable quality hand-held microphone can be very economical to purchase and simple to operate, although one must take care to keep them the correct distance from the mouth to keep sound even and prevent hissing, lisping sounds or breathiness. They are less easy to damage, and quick and easy to set up, but may interfere with hand movement, so can curb gestures or use of whiteboards or props.

Lavaliere microphones are small microphones that attach to the shirt or coat, to keep your hands free. They are reasonably inexpensive and small and easy to transport. Their drawback is that one must take care not to turn too far away from the microphone when speaking – if turning, do so from the waist, so the microphone moves with the mouth. Also, care must be taken with jewellery or other accessories, as they may bump against the microphone, interfering with the sound quality.

Headset microphones sit on the head to keep the hands completely free. Set up properly, they allow the speaker full freedom of movement, and constant sound quality. Care must be taken to keep the distance from the mouth to the received just right. Too far away and you'll be too quiet; too close and your audience will be treated to heavy breathing and a series of pft's and hisses. I recommend a skin tone receiver, in preference to the big black ball style, as this allows for maximum viewing of facial expressions.

Recently, there have been newer styles emerging, including a necklace style microphone which – like the name – fastens around the neck, keeping the hands free. Again, this can be a problem when moving the head and the body must turn from the waist. Also, care must be taken not to drop the chin too much or the receiver can get buried under the chin and lose effectiveness.

A couple of things to note with microphones. The receiver is very sensitive. Knocking on the microphone to check if it is turned on is not recommended as it can cause damage to the receiver resulting in poor sound quality. To test if the microphone is working, simply say "testing one, two" – preferably before the audience arrives, but will be accepted by an audience who are probably happy you are on the stage and they are not!

When using a microphone, moving too close to the amplifier will create squealing feedback. If that happens, move away from the amplifiers. Standing directly in front or behind amplifiers can also have this effect.

For cordless headsets or hand microphones, be aware that if the receiver is analogue, it can be affected by any other radio transmission device in the area – including mobile phones and CB radios such as those used in trucks or taxis as they pass a building. Signal interference creates sound drop out – which can destroy a speech. When buying or hiring equipment, it is worth the added expense to purchase digital receivers to prevent this issue.

There is a tendency towards loud music during speaking events and during audience thinking time or work time during workshops. While music can add extra energy to the room, the presenter must be aware that some audience members find it very distracting to have music playing when they are trying to focus. This can affect their outcomes, so may lead to negative feedback on your events. Also, background music can affect the audience's ability to hear what is being said.

Visual

It seems these days a presentation is expected to include projected visual aid – whether via a data projector or a Television screen. Certainly, the use of PowerPoint, Prezi or Keynote for visual display is regarded as highly professional. But a poorly presented digital visual presentation can make the speaker look extremely unprofessional. If you are unable to seamlessly use data projection, you are better to not use it at all. If you are a novice, but learning, make sure you have a knowledgeable support person with you who can troubleshoot for you. When using a computer, be familiar with the workings of your computer, and allow enough advance time on arrival to test the equipment and ensure it works.

When using digital projection, it is imperative that the font and image sizes are large enough to be read at all ends of the room, not only on your computer screen when creating them. A too-small font will create an audience who simply stop trying to read it (hence is a waste of time and effort) or create a situation where the audience stops listening to try to read what is on the slide (making your words a waste).

Recently, I attended a networking event where the speaker's desired outcome was to get clients to sign up to a $400/hour coaching service. I met her prior to the event. She seemed a lovely lady, who connected easily with those she met and was very professional in her manner and communication ability. Her presentation was very professionally put together, with spectacular graphics but sadly, that is where it stopped. As soon as she was introduced, she turned her back and read every sentence of her presentation. She sold nothing that night and nobody signed up for more information about her services. Where did she go wrong?

Digitally projected images should be supporting information only – not the whole presentation – and the presenter most definitely should NOT turn and read off the slides – firstly because your voice disappears when you turn your back to your audience; secondly because you appear to be unfamiliar with the content if you have to read it all off the PowerPoint presentation; and thirdly because it looks like you think your audience is unable to read for themselves. As the speaker, you are the star of the show – the data projector is your back-up singer. Use your visuals only for back-up or to support or illustrate difficult to remember concepts such as timelines, graphs or data.

Slides should also include images in preference to text. Bullet points are boring and best avoided. Visual cues that stay with the listener are recommended – for example, if you are talking about a core component of a concept, use an apple core or similar image – it's a familiar and very memorable image and helps to embed the topic.

The final item to note when presenting with a data projector is to take care to not walk or stand between the projected data and the screen. If moving in front of the screen is unavoidable, use a presentation tool to block the light.

Some of the cleverest professional presentations I have witnessed did not include digitally projected data. Flipcharts have made a great resurgence lately and whiteboards are priceless in the way in which they allow the speaker to expand on a subject and include more detailed investigation or brainstorming to increase engagement and learning for the audience.

One of the most impressive flipchart presentations I ever saw was given by a financial planner. We were impressed with his ability to do long equations, explain compound interest and draw an accurate map of the Stock Market for the past 60 years. After the presentation, I went over to congratulate him and discovered all the information was already written on the flip chart in very light pencil! I wonder how many audience members signed up to his program that night, believing he was an absolute wizard with numbers!

Flip chart sheets can also be pinned around the room to remind attendees of their learnings or for continued addition over a period of days during a long event.

When using a whiteboard or flipchart, make sure you are using the correct pen. If you accidentally use a permanent marker on a whiteboard, take a whiteboard pen and go over the permanent maker lines with it, then clean off the result – the whiteboard pen will dissolve the permanent marker. Do not use methylated spirit on a whiteboard as it destroys the surface finish and whilst the board will appear clean, it will not clean properly with future use and will become quite grey and difficult to read.

Whiteboard pens should not be used on flipcharts as they seep through the paper and mark the sheet behind, and they'll run out very quickly – they are more watery than permanent markers and are specifically designed for use on non-porous surfaces.

Whether using a flipchart or a whiteboard, make sure the font is large enough to be read all through the room. Also, block letters are recommended to assist with legibility, and care should be taken when using colour to ensure it does not fade into obscurity from the back of the room.

Gadgets

Interactive tablets with a stylus, such as the Wacom can also be used to do free-hand explanations and displays. These gadgets can be plugged into the computer allowing for handwritten or drawn graphics to be displayed immediately. This is very useful in cases where a whiteboard cannot be sourced, or when travelling to speak or present.

Infra-red pointers are useful for pointing out data on digitally projected screens but can disappear on LED or Plasma TV Screens. In these cases, an extending pointer stick may be needed – they may be old fashioned, but they are still effective!

Presentation tools for advancing slides are recommended and often include a built-in pointer and timing device, which can be very useful. Often referred to as 'clickers', these tools come in a variety of shapes and sizes.

There is even a new one, only recently available, that fits on your finger and is not at all obvious when speaking. I recommend you try a few out to find the one that fits best to your hand shape and user preference.

These implements generally have a small USB receiver which must be plugged into your computer to receive information from the hand-held device. Often, they

Operate Devices

only work if the slides have been set to slideshow presentation mode.

When using a clicker, position the computer screen so you can easily see what slide you are up to at a quick glance. When advancing slides, aim the clicker at the computer to press, not at the screen (you'd be surprised how many people do that). Try to keep your slide forwarding surreptitious and maintain the flow of your speaking while you change slides. Remember to use the blank out button to turn off the images when you want the audience to focus intently on you, or when you need to walk across the screen.

When holding pens, pointers or any other gadget, try not to fiddle with it while speaking as this can get distracting to your audience. The general rule of thumb is if you are not using it, put it down. However, if you are someone who loses what you put down, you are better to hold on to it in preference to disrupting the presentation while you search for it.

Props

On occasion, you may wish to demonstrate a real-life item. When doing this, bear in mind the size of the item — a very large item may need to be pre-placed in front of the room; a smaller item may need to be handed around in order to be seen. When holding up a prop for display, take care not to block the face by holding the item to the side. Also, ensure the item is at a height appropriate level, so all present can see it.

Reflection

Where could you get opportunities to practice using audio visual equipment?

What is the biggest area of learning you need to undertake to feel using AV is simple?

What kinds of presentations have you done?

What other kinds of presentations could you do?

Action

Rent or buy a cheap microphone and amplifier and practice speaking with it so you can get used to using one.

Familiarise yourself with the display settings on your computer.

Practice setting up slide shows and using a clicker to advance slides while speaking.

Practice writing on a whiteboard or flipchart.

Practice speaking with a prop in front of a mirror, so you know how to hold it where it doesn't block the way.

BECOME CALM   ACQUIRE SKILLS   LIBERATE VOICE   LET IT FLOW   OWN THE SPACE   OPERATE DEVICES   NURTURE PROGRESS

Step Seven

Nurture Progress

> *"It behoves every man to remember that the work of the critic is of altogether secondary importance, and that, in the end, progress is accomplished by the man who does things."*
> **Theodore Roosevelt**

Any learning journey comes with challenges and there will be times when you feel discouraged. Remember that the journey to mastery (Unconscious competence) requires passage through the discomfort of realising how much you have yet to learn. We must embrace the discomfort and never give up.

It is a very strong-minded human who does not feel discouraged at times. To protect and nurture one-self along the journey, I recommend finding a team of like-minded positive individuals who will give you strength when yours is low through showing support.

I have previously mentioned POWERtalk Australia — a not-for-profit organisation that assists through provision of a safe space in which to practice. But practice alone is not enough. You must also get feedback which encourages your journey as well as showing the next area of focus for growth. This is where POWERtalk truly shines!

Members are trained to evaluate and give supportive feedback as part of any meeting — this is a rare and beautiful opportunity to leap ahead when learning to speak. We cannot see ourselves when we are speaking. To be given the honest opinion of an audience member is invaluable in learning what we are doing well, and where we are simply not connecting. Even after 15 years of speaking, I still run new talks through at club meetings to get feedback on their effectiveness.

The thing to remember about feedback is that it is one person's impression. There are many who will tell you to keep a positive mindset and simply ignore negative feedback. If the feedback is simple trolling, that is most definitely the recommended approach, however not all negative feedback is trolling.

When you receive feedback that is less than positive, take the time to objectively examine it. Ask people you respect and know will be straight with you for additional opinions. If the negative feedback is repeated, there is probably an issue that needs rectification.

I note here that new concepts can often bring resistance — there are wet blankets everywhere! Decide if the negative feedback is simply resistance to change and be prepared to stick to your guns if this is the case. To achieve your desired outcome, you may need to restructure your proposal, or perhaps clarify steps and put strategies in place to handle objections.

Speaking as a Sustainable Business

Very few people who make money from speaking do so by speaking alone. So-called 'speaking businesses' usually do not only sell products created through speaking – such as being hired to emcee events or ceremonies; speaking as a keynote or motivational speaker; running workshops, seminars and other training, both face to face and online; podcasts, radio and television; and sales of recorded speaking such as DVD, CD, or online hosted recordings either on YouTube or other hosted media. Income from these products is usually backed up by other non-speaking products such as books, planners, diaries or journals.

To create a speaking business, one must grow their profile to become a speaker in demand by being very visible. In addition to being seen through standard marketing and promotional activities, this often requires a good deal of attendance and performances at networking and industry events, summits and seminars, often for little or no income, and sometimes at personal cost.

This is all part of the game – the big money will not come to someone who has not yet proved their value in this industry. If you want to be the next big thing in speaking, you must be prepared to put in the hours and effort to get known in your field.

Funnels

A clear business structure is vital. Funnels are the most common business marketing tool used by professional speakers. Below is a diagram of a typical professional speakers' business funnel.

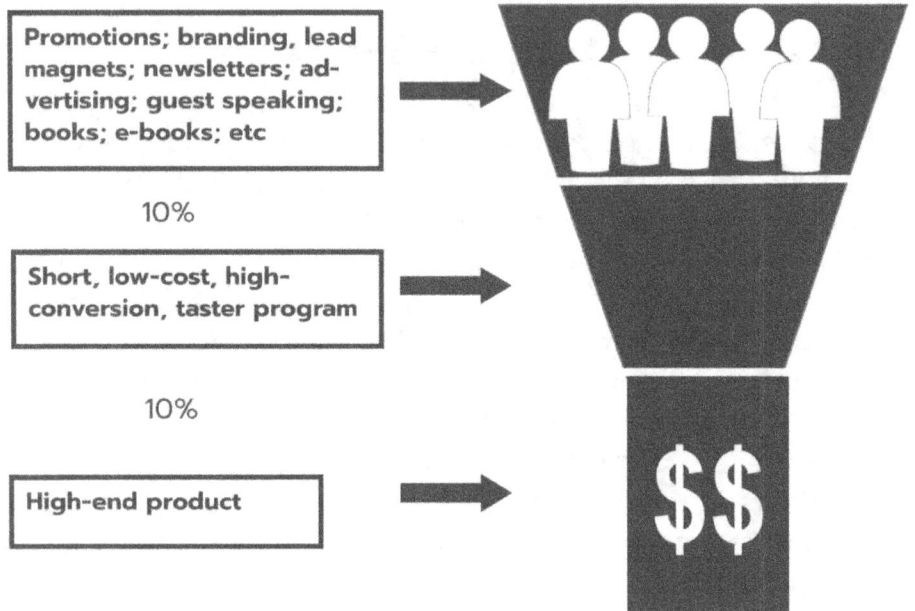

Whilst the funnel in this image represents a three-tiered funnel, the speaker's business model may include several three-tiered funnels; many more tiers to the one funnel; or a combination of both.

In a multi-tiered funnel, the first tier focuses on creating awareness. The speaker is promoted heavily in order to gain visibility - often delivering free of charge.

The second level consists of a short, low or no cost speaking event, at which the speaker demonstrates their ability and knowledge in their chosen subject. At this event, attendees are offered a higher-level product, usually a training course or guided coaching program at a much greater cost – i.e. a high-end product.

The usual and anticipated conversion rate for speaking events is around 10%, meaning that at each level, only 1/10 of those who attend an event will buy up to the next level. Most of the marketing and promotion budget is spent at the top of the funnel. Therefore, it follows, that if one can structure a presentation in such a manner that the customers are excited and well-served with a resultant conversion rate increase, there is a subsequent and significant saving to be made in promotional costs.

For example, if you have 1000 people at the top of the funnel, the anticipation in 100 people will attend the mid-level event and around 10 people will purchase the higher-level offering.

If you could double the conversion rate, you would get 20 people purchasing the higher-level offering for the same promotional costs, effectively halving the cost per person who attends, and doubling your profits.

An excellent mid-level product can consistently convert around 70% of attendees, creating a 700% improvement in income – well worth the effort of improving the presentation!

Hence the focus must be on increasing conversions from the mid-level program, through specifically targeted presentations.

Clearly understanding your audience and their needs (and delivering tailored products to fulfil those needs) is vital to your success. Without a clear understanding of who is in your audience, their pain points, and what they require from you in order to address those pain points, you will not succeed in making money from your speaking business. Not only should you tailor your presentation to those pain points, you should also promote your products with advertising directed to address those pain points, creating a higher rate of conversion to your higher-level programs. Remember, it's all about your audience, and if the people you have in your room already want what you have to offer, your job will be far easier.

Speaking as Leadership

The keys to success in any type of leadership are Fortitude, alignment, service, vision, and strategy.

You must have the guts to stick with it, to take on the hard tasks and the difficult people. Learning people skills and general conversational skills will make a big difference to your success. Emotional intelligence is a big part of this – find ways to personify the leaders you most admire. Learn the skills to stay calm and respond, rather than react, to any situations that arise with dignity and integrity.

Remain aligned to your cause – people recognise misalignment and their trust of you as a leader is diminished when they see inauthentic behaviour. If you don't have trust, you won't have buy-in. Your followers will leave, and you will not get speaking opportunities.

Speaking is a gift – not in the sense that you have a gift for speaking. Rather in the sense that when you speak, you are imparting a gift to your audience – you are in service to them when you inform, inspire or persuade them. Leadership is service, not ego. When you are caught in making yourself feel good, you are serving your ego, not your audience. Spend your energy looking after them, and you will deliver a more heart-felt and impactful message.

Keep a clear vision of your desired outcome. There will always be someone who doesn't believe – in fact, if your idea is ground-breaking, there is often many people who don't believe in it, especially to start with. Be prepared for the flack – breathe deep, stand strong and don't give up.

As in any situation where you wish to make progress, strategy is required. Being visible is vital to success as a speaker – you must be prepared to be seen and spoken about. Perceptions are all-important to gaining opportunities to speak out. If nobody knows who you are, nobody will want to create an event where you appear.

Becoming visible requires strategic positioning and planning. There is no such thing as an overnight success – the person who was in the right place at the right time for the breakthrough had, without a doubt, been strategically working towards that position for quite some time – sometimes a whole lifetime.

Your strategy must include being prepared to step up and share the vision, regardless of the flack. If you wish to be a world-changing, leading speaker, you must first do the work on yourself. The effect of personal development cannot be underestimated – mindset, emotional intelligence, communication skills and your ability to connect intelligently with the right people are all vital components of becoming a speaker of renown. Nurturing progress must include these components.

Allowing yourself to speak out, step up, and shine can be exhausting. Learn to implement boundaries which leave space for relaxation and rejuvenation. Just as the best car requires maintenance so do you! When you are exhausted your performance drops, your immune system is affected and your ability to think clearly diminishes. In this space, you are more likely to come undone in front of an audience with mind blanks or difficulty in enunciation or articulating sentences. Meditation is a brilliant tool for rejuvenation but cannot be used in isolation. You must also be careful to ensure adequate rest, hydration and nutrition.

The right support team is also very necessary. Once you become well-known, there are so many demands on your time, self-care may seem an impossibility. Put the structures in place to support your journey before you get very well-known.

Speaking as a business requires all the same business support principles as any other business. Create your policies and procedures and maintain them with regular updating. Create your base administration processes, remembering to pay attention to finance, marketing, promotion and sales as well as growth, teamwork and professional development for all team members.

Get clear about what the journey entails – you do that by first being curious and asking lots of questions... what would it take for this change to happen? What would it take for me to get the message out? What else is out there already working towards the same purpose? What do I need to do differently to what is already being done? What do I need to do differently in my own life to make me able to perform this mission? What else do I need to know or do?

Remember to take a whole brain approach and look at this from every angle, not only your favoured thinking style.

When you have clarity about what is required, it's time to move into project management mode. First map a plan – this may be a visual model, a mind map, a spreadsheet, a wall full of post-it notes or an online program. Whatever mode you use must be the one that works for your own style of processing. Add a timeline to your plan.

Remember that we often overestimate what we can achieve in a short space of time and underestimate what we can achieve long term. Build your plan on that premise and be happy to flex things forward in preference to putting them off. This will help you to avoid overwhelm and procrastination which often comes when you overestimate your ability to achieve things in a specific timeframe.

Next commit, schedule and diarise specific sessions in which to complete this plan. Structure time into your schedule for maintaining the organisation of your space, for admin duties, for networking and meetings, for professional development, for the special people in your life and for time out, fun, exercise, relaxation and self-care. If you do not schedule these things, life will overtake your project and it will not happen. Use your time wisely and you will find you will get ahead of your plan with remarkable ease and feel good while doing it too.

As your mission grows and evolves, you will find it impossible to do it all. Rather than wait until you get to that point, be proactive in sourcing the right people for your team – be on the lookout for professionals who share your values. When you work with people who have aligned values it is far easier to work through issues or conflicts that arise, as you all want the same thing underneath the surface.

The temptation may be to continue to work alone, especially if you are someone who finds it difficult to manage others. If that is the case, consider employing a manager and allow yourself to be the founder and visionary leader while your manager keeps it all going in the background for you. We all know that if you put twenty sticks together you create a strength far greater than 20 times the strength of one stick. It works the same with people. Grow and align your team and you will soar.

Now, it's time. Drive the mission. Get out there in the public eye. Be prepared to give freely of yourself while you grow your following, but also have products in place that create income. You must be well-known with an excellent reputation before you can expect high income from simply speaking. So, as you become known, remember to work towards proving that you have value to give.

Writing a book is a good way to leverage into speaking and get known. In addition, employ social media strategies to become better known, attend networking events, grow a following, apply to speak at summits, conferences and other events. Keep at it, even when it feels like you are getting nowhere...because there will be times when it does feel that way!

Throughout it all, remember that we all have good days and bad days. That no matter what level you are at, there will be times when you question yourself and your ability to complete the mission. Never make a big decision about the course of the mission when you are having a bad day. Focus on the problem at hand and save the big decisions for a day when you are not feeling overwhelmed or unsure.

Nurture Progress

When you face a big issue, chunk it down into smaller pieces. Work through the problem and put steps in place to mitigate recurrent issues in future, always remembering that working through difficulty makes us stronger, and our mission clearer. Be prepared to move with the flow – you've got this!

Part Four

Paying It Forward

If you want to truly embody the learning you have received, the best way is to pay it forward through assisting others who are up and coming in your field. Isaac Newton famously said, "If I have seen further it is by standing on the shoulders of giants." In this quote he speaks of having mentors, advisers who helped him along his journey. Can you imagine how much those mentors learnt from Isaac?

If you wish to see further, get a mentor, if you wish to extend yourself further, be a mentor. This is where you will start your legacy.

Creating a legacy of Change

To me, legacy means leaving a positive mark on the world – creating something that positively affects the generations that follow. If you believe you are here for a purpose, then you have a legacy to leave. For some, that sounds too big, but I see it as three simple keys.

The Balloon Principle

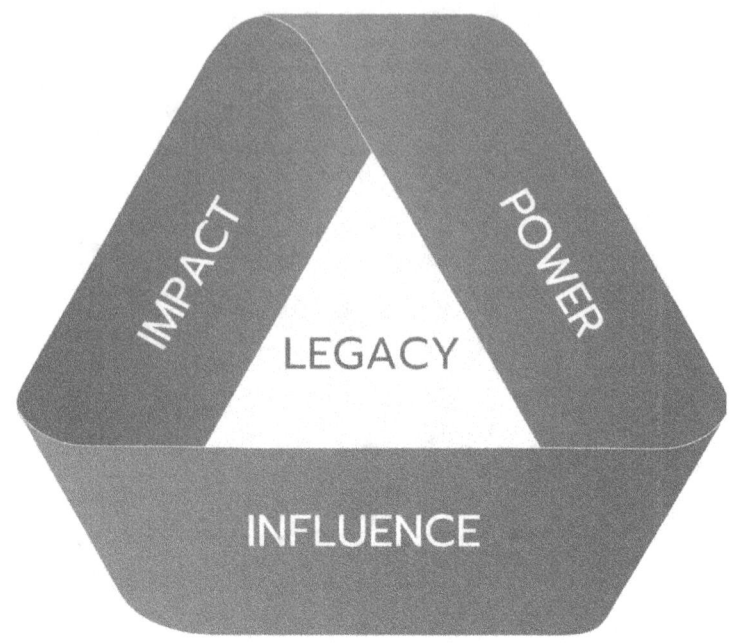

My formula for creating a legacy is:

POWER + INFLUENCE + IMPACT = LEGACY

In this instance 'power' does not refer to hierarchical power. Instead, it refers to personal power – the ability to stand in your own power, to rise to a challenge, to stick with your vision and mission, to be the person you were designed to be. Be true to you and embrace that personal power.

Influence is created through living true to your vision and mission; through controlling yourself, not others; through allowing those around you to feel appreciated, respected and valued; by assisting others to grow and shine; through service.

As Marianne Williamson says (slightly paraphrased), "When you shine you unconsciously give others permission to shine". Stand up and be you, embracing the purpose of this life you have been given, and people will be drawn to follow you.

Impact requires effort. Work hard at your cause and apply strategic plans to effect real change. Start small and work your way up – sometimes the smallest things make a huge difference. Look for small ways that will leapfrog your cause forward and allow those around you to see that you have impact. When that happens, you grow momentum and can effect much bigger change.

And that, my friends, is how you can speak out, step up and shine, so you leave the legacy you were put here for.

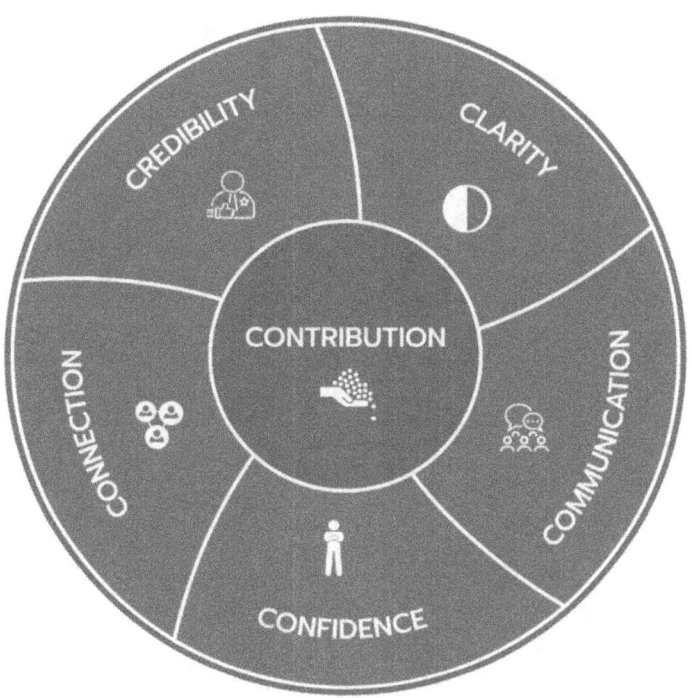

Remember, if you can connect and communicate your vision with clarity and credibility, and underpin all of that with confidence, you have everything you need to make the contribution you wish to make to this world.

Next Steps

So now you know what's needed, where to from here?

Practice:
POWERtalk Australia – Most clubs allow three free meetings so you can see if it's a fit for you. Find a club near you at www.powertalkaustralia.org.au/find-a-club-near-you

Workshops:
Balloon Principle Speaker Masterclass workshops are held around Australia and New Zealand. As a purchaser of this book, you are entitled to a low-cost ticket – use the code BPBOOK to access your low-cost ticket. To find a workshop near you, go to www.optimalcoaching.com.au/events

Mentoring:
I cannot recommend mentoring highly enough. I still have mentors who I regularly run things by. Being able to bounce ideas and concepts off people whose opinion and experience you respect is priceless.

Ask about mentoring sessions, learning to become a mentor through Optimal Life Solutions, or to enquire about what fits best for you by getting in contact with me at https://optimalcoaching.com.au/contact

About the Author

Mary Wong is an international speaker and trainer, having spoken around the globe in USA, Canada, United Kingdom, Asia and the Pacific to rave reviews.

She created the Balloon Principle ® signature speaking system and presents training for entrepreneurs, corporations and not-for-profit organisations in Australia, New Zealand and throughout Asia, as well as working cybernetically with high-level clients worldwide.

It is Mary's personal journey that proves to her that the ability to be an exceptional communicator can be learned. She says her mission is to help people with bright ideas to find their voice and make a difference to the world.

The Balloon Principle is her second book. Her first, a compilation, Voices of the 21st Century II, released in September 2019 with Gail Watson and the Women's Speakers Association, shot to international Best Seller status in four categories, remaining in the top ten best sellers list for more than a week on Amazon in four countries.

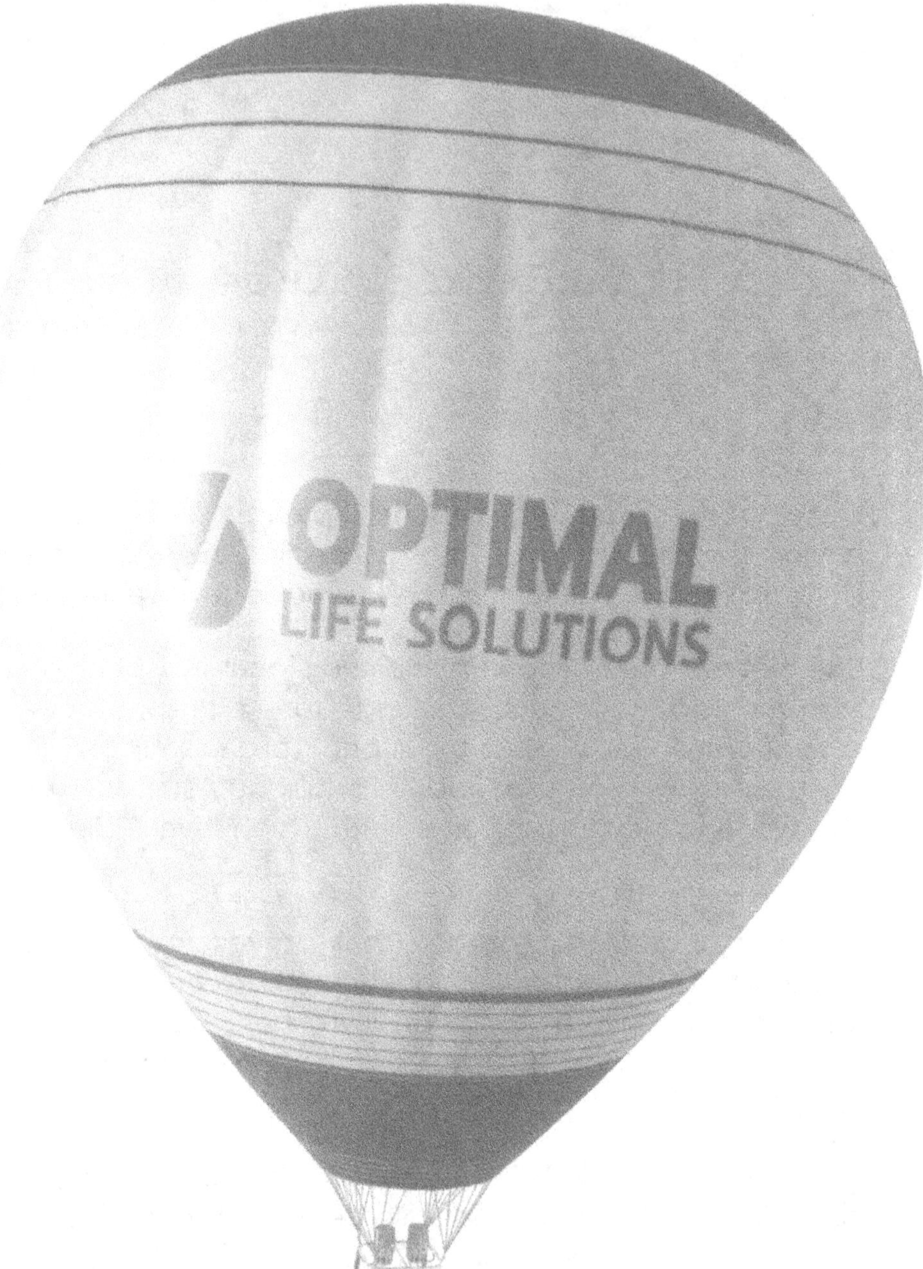
OPTIMAL
LIFE SOLUTIONS

www.ingramcontent.com/pod-product-compliance
Lightning Source LLC
Chambersburg PA
CBHW071349080526
44587CB00017B/3026